The Lewis and Clark Expedition

The Lewis and Clark Expedition
Food, Nutrition, and Health

by Elaine Nelson McIntosh, Ph.D., R.D.
University of Wisconsin at Green Bay

The Center for Western Studies
Augustana College
2003

Published by The Center for Western Studies
Mailing address: Box 727, Augustana College, Sioux Falls, SD 57197
Street address: Augustana College, 2201 S. Summit Ave., Sioux Falls, SD 57197
E-mail address: cws@augie.edu
Copies of our book catalog may be obtained by calling 605-274-4007 or by visiting our web page at
www.augie.edu/CWS.

The Center for Western Studies is an archives, library, museum, publishing house, and educational agency con-
cerned principally with collecting, preserving, and interpreting prehistoric, historic, and contemporary materials that document native and immigrant cultures on the northern prairie-plains. The Center promotes
understanding of the region through exhibits, publications, art shows, conferences, and academic programs. It
is committed, ultimately, to defining the contribution of the region to American civilization.

Library of Congress Cataloging-in-Publication Data

McIntosh, Elaine N.
    The Lewis and Clark expedition : food, nutrition, and health aspects / by Elaine Nelson McIntosh.
       p. cm. -- (Prairie plains series ; no. 9)
    Includes bibliographical references and index.
    ISBN 0-931170-80-X
      1. Lewis and Clark Expedition (1804-1806) 2. Wilderness survival. 3. Outdoor
life--Health aspects. 4. Explorers--West (U.S.)--History--19th century. 5. Mountaineering
injuries. I. Title. II. Series.

RC88.9.05M255 2003
613.6'9--dc21   2002041724

Cover image of Spirit Mound by South Dakota Tourism. Inset image of the Death Camas and Blue Camas by Drs.
Nancy J. and Robert D. Turner.

Publication was made possible in part with a grant from the Mellon Fund Committee of Augustana College.

Number 9 in the Prairie-Plains Series

Printed in the United States of America
by Pine Hill Press, Inc.
4000 W. 57th St.
Sioux Falls, SD 57106

Table of Contents

Preface

My interest in the Lewis and Clark Expedition began while writing *American Food Habits in Historical Perspective* (Praeger, 1995). While doing research for this book, I came across considerable information regarding explorers and the food problems they often faced. And I was reminded of something that health professionals have known for a long time—that certain groups of people tend to be at special risk for malnutrition, i.e., soldiers, sailors, and explorers—people on expeditions of all kinds. Food problems frequently arise, because the travelers usually have left their native habitats and are now in unfamiliar, often adverse, situations, without the usual supports and infrastructures which encourage a dependable food supply. Malnutrition, of course, results in impaired functioning, as well as various nutritionally-related disorders. In addition, it lowers one's resistance to various diseases.

I found myself becoming very interested in this group of people. But I did not have space in my 1995 book to go into any detail regarding the special challenges they faced with respect to food, nutrition, and health. Finally, I dealt with this dilemma by promising myself that some day I would write about these special challenges that face expeditions. Little did I realize then how very soon that would happen.

Only three weeks later, in January of 1996, I received a mailing from the Center for Western Studies at Augustana College, Sioux Falls (my alma mater), asking for abstracts for the upcoming Dakota History Conference, whose theme would be "Exploration of the Northern Plains." I presented a paper at the conference that May on the role of food in the exploration of the northern plains, with special emphasis on the Lewis and Clark Expedition. It was well received, and I found myself inspired to examine the expedition in greater depth. As a result, I have been reading and writing about the food, nutrition, and health aspects of that epic journey ever since. This book is the first to examine these three parameters as interrelated, critical factors in the outcome of the expedition.

As I read the literature and—through the journals—followed the Corps of Discovery, I became increasingly appreciative of the party's compelling need to obtain food from the land, daily. Important though their weapons and ammunition and other supplies were, adequate food was really the *sine qua non* of the undertaking. There have been many failed endeavors in the annals of history that attest to that fact. Numerous explorers and pioneers have set out, never to return, because of starvation. Much has been written about the Lewis and Clark Expedition, but most of the literature has focused on its geographical, political, and diplomatic aspects. In these works, the need for food often seems to be accepted as a given. The party's medical and health problems, in general, tend to be under-emphasized. Dr. Eldon Chuinard's book *Only One Man Died: The Medical Aspects of the Lewis and Clark Expedition* (1979) made a land-mark contribution to the existing literature regarding the medical aspects of the expedition. But, although he included some information regarding the party's nutritional deficiencies, he did not address the party's nutritional problems or status in any depth. Dr. Bruce Paton, in *Lewis & Clark: Doctors in the Wilderness* (2001), provides new insights regarding the medical aspects of the trip, but hardly mentions the nutritional aspects of the venture.

In the present book, I have attempted to provide an extensive analysis of the expedition from the standpoint of food, nutrition, and health within the context of current dietary knowledge. Included are a discussion of the status of medicine during this period, the various advantages accruing to the party from wintering at Camp Dubois prior to departure up the Missouri, the party's inability to tolerate the camas root at Weippe Prairie in 1805, fluctuations in game availability, the epidemic of contagious diseases while at Fort Clatsop, and, finally, a comprehensive health-related analysis of the party based on available vital statistics and other information about the men. I hope that this book will serve as a positive contribution to the existing literature.

While following this epic journey, I feel that I, too, have been experiencing a unique personal venture.

Acknowledgments

The author wishes to express her appreciation to the many individuals and organizations which helped make this book possible: Drs. Arthur Huseboe and Harry Thompson, and the staff at the Center for Western Studies, for their invaluable help, advice, and support; the librarians at the University of Wisconsin-Green Bay, who assisted me in obtaining books via Inter-library Loan; Drs. Nancy J. and Robert D. Turner, at the University of Victoria, who provided the Camas images, and Dr. Steve Dutch, at the University of Wisconsin-Green Bay, for his cartographic assistance in map preparation. Special thanks go to the many persons who provided helpful background material, including Drs. Joyce and V. Ronald Nelson and Dr. Evelyn Peterson. The author is especially grateful to her husband, Dr. Tom McIntosh, for his patience, assistance, and unfailing support throughout the preparation of this book.

Introduction

During the summer of 1802, President Jefferson and Meriwether Lewis had read with great interest Alexander Mackenzie's account of his 1792-1793 voyage to the Pacific.[1] Mackenzie and his party had made it to the Pacific, traversing Canadian territory. But, almost immediately, the party had returned to Fort Chipewyan, at Lake Athabasca. For Jefferson and Lewis, Mackenzie's expedition served as a competitive stimulus for them to accomplish something bigger and better for their own country.

It is difficult to envision any better way whereby Jefferson and Lewis could have readied themselves for their anticipated expedition than by studying the journals of Mackenzie.[2] The perils and problems that Mackenzie and his party encountered, and how they dealt with them, served as an excellent guide in preparing and executing a similar, American undertaking. The challenges which these Canadians had faced included food scarcity, physical danger and exertions, illness, rain and inclement weather, as well as problems associated with their Indian guides, and dealing with other Indians which they met en route. The Lewis and Clark Expedition encountered many similar situations.

This book focuses on the diet and health aspects of the Lewis and Clark party throughout the expedition. As a basis for making dietary assessments, the author has used the current food guide advocated by the United States Department of Agriculture, Human Nutrition Information Service.[3] It is called the Six Food Group Plan (Table 1.1), sometimes presented as a graphic and known as the Food Guide Pyramid.[4] These six food groups provide the nutrients required by the body for proper functioning. The sixth food group, for example, includes fats, concentrated sweets, and alcoholic beverages. They should be used sparingly; fats—as well as some sugars—are already obtained from the other food groups. Alcohol provides energy as calories, but contains essentially no nutrients. Three of the food groups (breads/cereals, fruits, and vegetables) also provide fiber, needed for normal intestinal activity and elimination. The table also lists the recommended ranges of servings for each food group. The exact number of servings needed for a given person depends upon the individuals's age, size, level of activity, and other factors.

Using this plan, I have assessed the typical diets during Colonial times and the early years of the new Republic, and, also, the diets of the Lewis and Clark party, as they experienced changing food availabilities (with respect to both types and amounts) throughout the expedition. Since the men were quite large and active, the recommended numbers of servings would have been at the high end of the range for each food group listed. Using this guide, I have made qualitative (and semi-quantitative) assessments of the men's diets, including mineral and vitamin intakes, based on information regarding food consumption found in the journals.

Like most Americans during the early years of the Republic, the members of the Lewis and Clark Expedition at the time of their recruitment undoubtedly had dietary histories which were far from ideal. Their intakes of riboflavin, vitamin C, vitamin E, folic acid, calcium, iodine, and fiber probably had been low. Water consumption, too, tended to be low during this era. These nutrient deficiencies were caused mainly by the lack of fruits, vegetables, and milk. Unfortunately, most of these dietary lacks became exacerbated during the expedition because of the continued lack of these foods, as well as eggs. Indeed, during periods of food scarcity, the party suffered from inadequate food (and calories) *per se*. Usually, however, the men were consuming adequate protein, fats, and carbohydrates. At times, the men actually were consuming too much fat and protein, which would have placed a strain on the gastrointestinal system, liver, and kidneys.

Throughout the expedition, there was a persistent pattern of even lower intakes of riboflavin, vitamins C and E, folic acid, and calcium, plus fiber and water. The nutritional status of the men was compromised further by the stresses of the trip, since stress increases the excretion of virtually all the nutrients. Their dietary deficits, together with the rigors of the trip and the various injuries incurred, resulted in increasing health problems as the undertaking progressed.

The Corps of Discovery arrived back at St. Louis on September 22, 1806, after an absence of twenty-eight months. Only one man had died. However, the deteriorating health of the men and their decreasing ability to function would have curtailed the expedition had it continued much longer.

Chapter 1
Diet and Health in the Colonies and New Republic

The members of the Lewis and Clark Expedition were products not only of the early years of the Republic (1783-1803), which had immediately preceded this undertaking, but also of the late Colonial Period (1763-1783). Therefore, it seems appropriate to provide a brief overview of the status of both diet and health during each of these periods.

The foremost nutritional problem facing the earliest European settlers in North America was simply the obtaining of adequate food. Undernutrition, malnutrition, famine, and starvation were frequent threats. But once the colonists (with the help of the Indians) learned what food was available and how to get it and cook it, the supply became plentiful. In fact, the colonists kept themselves better supplied with food than any other people in the world at that time.[1]

Most of the colonists lived on farms, where they became reasonably self-sufficient by raising grain, cattle, hogs, sheep, chickens, fruits, and vegetables. By hunting, they obtained deer, wild turkeys, and other game. Those who lived near rivers or the ocean were able to obtain fish and shellfish of both freshwater and marine origin. The colonists soon began to grow the Indian staple, corn, which could be stored easily. Corn became a basic component of their diet. And, like the Indians, they ground it into cornmeal and prepared it in various ways. Most generally, it was made into variations of corn bread. But some corn was converted into corn hominy, or roasted.

In addition to corn bread, rye or wheat bread was made with yeast. These breads were usually baked in a small oven that was built into the fireplace, or outside the house against the hot chimney. The colonists also baked bread in an iron bake kettle, which had a tight-fitting lid. Meat or game was usually mixed with vegetables into a stew and cooked in a large iron pot that hung over the fire on a pothook, fastened to a crane or a chimney bar. The iron pot had short legs and sometimes was placed on a bed of coals. Whole fowl or large cuts of meat were often roasted on sharp-pointed rods called spits. Handles on the spits allowed the meat to be turned above the fire.[2] Sometimes fish or meat was broiled outdoors on wooden frames over a blazing fire.

The diet varied markedly by season and climate. Since the colonists did not yet have methods of canning or refrigeration, storing food for the winter was a problem. Some meat (especially pork) could be successfully salted or smoked, while certain vegetables were dried or pickled. Root vegetables and certain fruits (e.g., apples) were kept in cool, dry cellars. Generally, fresh fruit and vegetables were scarce. Bread and meat tended to be the standbys during winter.[3] Maple syrup and maple sugar were common sweeteners in the Northeast. According to C. Van Syckle, "The diet at times, particularly in winter, must have had little variety, but there seems to have been relatively little actual want."[4] By the 1700s, tea, coffee, and hot chocolate were popular beverages.[5]

An Anglo-American cuisine now developed. At its core was familiar, bland English cooking, with few spices, to which new accents were added. The colonists began to use a great deal of sugar, both in desserts and other dishes, particularly after 1750.[6] When sugar cane was brought to Louisiana in 1751, the cane sugar industry began in the colonies,[7] and soon the colonists became independent regarding their sugar supply. In fact, after 1750, Americans and Britons soon possessed the Atlantic world's greatest sweet tooth, with Americans running a close second to Englishmen in per capita sugar consumption.[8]

Most of the early colonists were shorter than Americans today. This situation can be deduced from the fact that European males during the late seventeenth and early eighteenth centuries were 2 to 4 inches shorter than 68 inches, the norm in the United States in 1982.[9] Therefore, it seems certain that first generation colonists from Europe during that period generally were of similar stature. Judging by the subsequent overall rise in stature in America from colonial times to the present, the diets of early settlers must have been limiting, at least with respect to certain key nutrients.

Using the Six Food Group Plan as a basis for dietary assessment (Table 1.1), we can conclude that the colonists were eating sufficient bread products, most commonly made from whole grains. This high consumption of whole-grain cereal products provided carbohydrate, some fiber, several of the B-vitamins, and some minerals. Root vegetables, which could be stored (e.g., sweet potatoes and carrots), were usually available, providing some vitamin A. But one of the main deficiencies of the colonial diet was its lack of fresh vegetables and fruits, which were largely seasonal. And, even when available, fresh vegetables were used sparingly in sauces and garnishes to accompany the meat dish, according to British custom. With the low intake of fresh fruits and vegetables, diets tended to be low in certain vitamins and minerals, particularly vitamin C, folic acid, and riboflavin. Fiber intake also was insufficient. Once they became familiar with hunting and the raising of livestock in America, most colonists enjoyed a dependable meat supply and, as a result, were obtaining sufficient protein and niacin. Pork was consumed mainly as salt pork since salt served as an excellent and readily available preservative.[10] Pork provided needed thiamin, and some riboflavin, in addition to protein and fat. Because milk consumption generally was low, dietary intake of calcium was inadequate, and the deficit in riboflavin became more pronounced. The colonial diet tended to be high in fat, salt, and sugar. For those who did not consume salt-water fish or other sea foods, iodine deficiency (and thus, endemic goiter) was common. Water intake was low. This dietary assessment is summarized in Table 1.2, column 1. The colonists drank large amounts of beer, cider, rum, or wine with all their meals rather than water. Like most Europeans of the day, they believed that their water was unsafe to drink. Although they themselves were heavy drinkers, British visitors to the colonies were astonished by the amount of liquor Americans drank.[11] Presumably, the Americans' consumption of alcohol considerably surpassed theirs. The colonists were well-acquainted with the production and use of alcoholic beverages, both fermented and distilled. However, their favorite alcoholic beverage was Madeira wine, imported from the Portuguese island of the same name.

By today's standards, the health of the colonists was poor. Most people suffered frequently from various illnesses, which they did not know how to treat or prevent. Many of the early settlements had been completely depopulated by epidemic diseases brought over from Europe, particularly smallpox. These ravaged settlements included the colonies at Jamestown and probably the "Lost Colony" at Roanoke Island[12] off the coast of what is now North Carolina. Epidemics of measles, diphtheria, typhoid fever, and yellow fever also occurred. In addition, such illnesses as dysentery, gout, influenza, pneumonia, rheumatism, scurvy and tuberculosis were common.[13] There was a scarcity of doctors and nurses during

Table 1.1— Six Food Group Plan[a]

Food Group[b]	Daily Servings[c]
Bread, cereals, and other grain products	6-11
Fruits	2-4
Vegetables	3-5
Meat, poultry, fish and alternates	2-3
Milk, cheese, and yogurt	2
Fats, concentrated sweets, and alcoholic beverages[d]	Use sparingly

a. USDA/HNS 1989.
b. These six food groups provide the nutrients required by the body for proper functioning.
c. Recommended ranges of servings for each food group. Exact number of servings needed for a given person will depend on the individual's age, size, level of activity, and other factors.
d. Foods in this category sometimes are called "Extras." They should be used in small amounts within individual calorie limits. Fats and sugars already are obtained from other food groups; alcohol provides energy as calories, but contains essentially no nutrients. Three of the food groups (breads/cereals, fruits, and vegetables) also provide fiber, needed for normal intestinal activity and elimination.

the colonial period. However, the poor medical care received by the colonists probably was no worse than that available to Europeans during this time. From all indications, low life expectancies, high death rates, and high birth rates prevailed during colonial times. Infant and fetal death rates were also high, approaching 50%.[14] But, during this same period, European health conditions were worse.[15] Smallpox continued to be a dread disease in the Continental armies, second only to camp fever, and was credited with a mortality rate of fifteen percent. Because of the gravity of this disease, Dr. Benjamin Rush, during the Revolutionary War, began to explore inoculation as a means of reducing the mortality rate, advocating that inductees be inoculated against smallpox upon entering the army. By this procedure, the mortality rate was reduced to one percent.[16] (Lewis had been inoculated with smallpox when he was in the army in 1795.)[17] Already aware of the potential danger to American Indians upon exposure to European diseases, President Thomas Jefferson wanted to prevent the transmission of smallpox to Indians with whom the expedition would come in contact going westward. Therefore, in his final instructions to Lewis on June 20, 1803, Jefferson specifically asked him to "carry with you some matter of the kine pox, inform those of them [the Indians] ...of its efficacy as a preservative from smallpox; & instruct them in the use of it."[18] Perhaps Jefferson also recognized that the Indians constituted a large potential sample, an excellent opportunity to perform a large-scale public health experiment. Unfortunately, the mass vaccinations never materialized. Lewis did carry with him a supply of the vaccine, as shown by his letter to President Jefferson mailed from Cincinnati, Ohio, October 3, 1803.[19] However, some experiments he had performed on the vaccine indicated that it "had lost its virtue." He asked Jefferson to send him some more, but, apparently, it was never sent.[20]

Eating habits during the early years of the Republic were very similar to those of the preceding Colonial period.[21] Probably because of the relatively few varieties of foods consumed by most British Americans before the mid-nineteenth century, a number of modern writers have viewed the diet of this era as monotonous and poorly prepared, as well as bland and heavy.[22] Herbs and spices were used sparingly. Much of the food was fried, and the left-over grease often was used for making sauces and gravies.

During this period, the diet varied according to geographic region, season, and socioeconomic level. Rural and urban diets differed, as did racial and ethnic diets. Richard

Cummings states that "land was cheap and meat abundant in the America of 1789."[23] Most people lived on small farms. They produced their own food, except for sugar, salt, and spices which they obtained from the country general store.

Corn and potatoes, along with pork, bread, and butter, comprised the basic American diet. These foods served as staples in the well-settled sections, as well as on the frontier. Corn was the main cereal grain in New England during this time, since wheat crops were often damaged by the "blast," a type of smut. As in colonial times, cornmeal was used in many ways.

White (Irish) potatoes were eaten in the North, while the sweet potato was the staple starch in the South. After harvesting in the autumn, the sweet potato could be fried, roasted, candied, or made into custard.

Pork was the favorite meat throughout the United States during this time, for several reasons. Pigs were allowed to roam free. They foraged for acorns and other fodder in forested areas, in all seasons, and required no attention at all.[24] Pork was valued not only for its excellent taste, but for its good keeping qualities. During this pre-refrigeration era, keeping most meats was a problem. But pork was unique in that it could be successfully preserved by smoking or salting, which actually improved its flavor.[25] These considerations obviously explain why salt pork was the only meat that Lewis and Clark took along on their voyage, augmenting it with jerky and pemmican, made en route (see Chapter 2). In the early nineteenth century, milk often was not available year-round in New England, because of open pasturage. Using this practice, which had been traditional in England, milk became scarce when grass became winterkilled.[26] Consequently, milk intake frequently was inadequate.

Milk that was not used immediately often was converted to butter and cheese in the homes, by means of churns and cheese presses. Unlike milk, cheese and butter could be kept for long periods. Even so, rancidity was a frequent problem, especially in dairy products. Milk was scarce in the South because of the difficulty of keeping it fresh in hot weather.[27]

During the early years of the Republic, fresh vegetables sometimes were served in season. But, as in Colonial times, they were used mainly as a side dish or "sass," in keeping with British tradition. Since leafy vegetables had poor keeping qualities, most of the vegetables consumed were those which could be stored in bins or preserved by drying. They included turnips, pumpkins, and beans. In the South, chickpeas were commonly eaten.[28]

In general, farmers had little fresh fruit. Since apples could be stored for several months, they were the most commonly eaten fruit in winter. In spring and summer, wild berries were available. Unfortunately, orchard fruits tended to be raised specifically for making cider and brandy.[29]

Some farmers on the coast drank tea or coffee and bought brown sugar or molasses (a by-product of the sugar industry) for sweetening.

Because the tobacco farmers of Virginia were single-cash croppers, they invested little time, energy, or land in the raising of food crops. Thus, both men and animals were "illy fed," according to Thomas Jefferson.[30]

At the beginning of the nineteenth century, methods of delivering foods to the markets were primitive. As a result, city dwellers had diets which were even lower in milk, fresh

Table 1.2—General Dietary Adequacy of Americans During the Late Colonial Period and Early Years of the Republic

Food Component	Late Colonial Period (ca. 1763-1783)	Early Years of Republic (1783-1803)
Water	—	—
Fiber	(—)	—
Total Calories	+	(+)
Carbohydrate	+	+
Fat	+	++
Protein	+	+
Vitamins		
Folic Acid	-	-
Niacin	+	(-)
Riboflavin	(-)	(-)
Thiamin	+	+
Vitamin B12	+	+
Vitamin C	-	-
Vitamin A (or carotene)	+	+
Vitamin D	(-)	(-)
Minerals		
Calcium	-	-
Magnesium	+	+
Phosphorus	+	+
Potassium	+	+
Sodium	+	++
Iodine	-	-
Iron	+	+
Copper	+	+
Manganese	+	+
Zinc	+	+

fruits, and vegetables than diets in the rural sector. Fresh milk and meat were scarce commodities. And, in summer, what fruits and vegetables were available sometimes were partially decomposed. Rancid, stale foods were common. But, despite the dietary shortcomings of city wage earners, they still were better fed than their European counterparts of this era.[31]

In urban, as well as in the rural areas, the most widely used meat was salt pork. Blood pudding was a commonly consumed by-product of butchering. Hog, or occasionally, beef blood, was mixed with chopped pork, then seasoned and stuffed in a casing. A pound of blood pudding could be bought for only three or four cents, which, along with butter crackers, could provide a meal for a hungry worker.[32]

Urban workers consumed large quantities of bread, one of the cheapest sources of energy. Potatoes also were an important staple. Because wheat was expensive, the poor in New England used corn, rye, or oat and barley meals for making bread.[33] City wage earners also tended to use molasses rather than sugar as a sweetener, since it was so much cheaper than the latter.[34]

In contrast to the modest wage earners, the more prosperous city people enjoyed much more varied diets. During the same period, a small percentage of the American rural population—wealthy land owners—were able to follow a cosmopolitan menu.[35]

At the beginning of the nineteenth century, the consumption of tea and coffee was about a pound per capita per annum. Tea still was the more popular of the two beverages in 1800. But by 1830, coffee had become uncontested as the prime American beverage.[36] This trend had begun with the onset of the Revolutionary War, when tea became politically unpopular, and later was reinforced by the War of 1812. The consumption of alcohol, mainly whiskey and other spirits, was high.[37]

In 1789, after the end of the Revolutionary War, life expectancy was 34.5 years for men and 36.5 for women (perhaps largely a reflection of high infant and child mortality rates).[38] By the late eighteenth century, the average stature of Americans had surpassed early Colonial levels. By the time of the American Revolution, native-born white males aged 34 to 35 measured 68.1 inches, which is virtually identical to heights in the United States Army during World War II.[39] This stature would suggest a fairly high level of nutrition. However, it is not known whether these men (presumably soldiers) were representative of the general population; young men from the more prosperous land-owning class may have been over-represented.

Based on current standards of dietary intake (Table 1.1), many people within both the rural and urban sectors during the early years of the Republic (Table 1.2, column 2) continued to have dietary deficiencies similar to those experienced during the late Colonial Period (Table 1.2, column 1). Bread, usually made from whole grains, was consumed in generous amounts. Meat consumption, for the most part, was adequate, as well. However, the most commonly used meat was salt pork, which is high in fat and low in the vitamin niacin. Corn, which was used in many ways, also is low in niacin. Low milk intake added to the niacin deficit, since milk contains the amino acid tryptophan, which can be converted to niacin in the body. Therefore, the diets of many people were likely to be quite low in this B-vitamin. Lack of niacin frequently leads to a deficiency disease known as pellagra, once a wide-spread public health problem in the South. Low milk intake also led to a lack of calcium and other minerals, plus other B-vitamins (e.g., riboflavin). Lack of fruits and vegetables also contributed to low intake of certain vitamins and minerals, particularly vitamin C, riboflavin, and folic acid. Thiamin intake probably was adequate, given the high consumption of pork and legumes (e.g., beans), as well as whole grain products. The low-fiber intake, associated with low consumption of fruits and vegetables and the relatively high consumption of meat, undoubtedly contributed to the wide-spread problem of constipation experienced by Americans of this period. Lack of fruits and vegetables, along with little milk, also would have resulted in the lack of numerous vitamins and minerals necessary for proper growth and maintenance of the body, as well as immunity from disease. These include riboflavin, vitamins A, C, and D, and the mineral calcium. Many Americans during this era were suffering from lack of vitamin C, unless they happened to be eating substantial amounts of potatoes and cabbage. (Nutritionists often refer to these two common foods as the "poor man's sources of vitamin C.") Undoubtedly, there were many subclinical, undiagnosed cases of scurvy during this era. Rickets was a common health problem among infants and children, because of the lack of vitamins A and D. Lack of milk and leafy green vegetables resulted in suboptimal intakes of calcium, riboflavin, and other vitamins and minerals necessary for proper growth and maintenance of the body. The result was reduced growth and stature. Lack of riboflavin also can cause eye problems ranging from sore, "runny" eyes to cataract formation, as well as various types of skin lesions, which were common afflictions.[40] Lack of the nutrients found in milk also may have contributed to the decayed, spotty, and missing teeth of both young and old.[41]

Urban workers and their families were less well fed than the rural population because they could raise little if any of their own food and had limited resources with which to buy what foods were available in the city at this time. City dwellers also were more likely to be deficient in vitamin D than rural people because they usually had less exposure to sunlight.

In addition to dietary deficiencies, there also were dietary excesses. In 1804, C. Volney noted that intakes of both fat and salt were high.[42] Particularly on the farms, people had access to large amounts of butter, fatty cheese, lard, and salted pork products, including hams and sausages. Despite the practice of soaking salt meat products before use, salt consumption still was too high. This salty diet encouraged the excessive use of sweeteners, since they were thought to "cut the salt" or mask its flavor.[43] It is regrettable that the relationship between high salt intake and high blood pressure was not recognized until the 1940s.

High intakes of sugar, fat, and salt had become common in the South, largely because of the abundance of pork produced on the plantations. High pork consumption led to high fat intake, and the need for salt to preserve this meat. Molasses (and, later, sugar), so readily available from the West Indies, was in high demand to mask the salty flavor of the pork. This pattern still prevails.[44]

Despite the high fat intake of many, obesity does not appear to have been common during the early years of the Republic. The most likely explanation is that total calorie intake was relatively moderate, considering the high level of physical activity of most Americans during this era, particularly on the farms.

Along the seacoast, breweries and cider mills provided beer and cider. However, these beverages tended to be scarce in the back country because of the lack of apples and facilities for keeping malt liquor. Instead, corn was fermented and distilled into whiskey, a popular drink among the pioneers.[45] According to Thomas Ashe, Kentuckians drank ardent spirits (strong distilled liquors) from morning to night.[46]

Waverly Root and Richard de Rochemont have indicated that "The drinking habits of the early nineteenth century were excessive."[47] High alcohol consumption appears to have continued until 1825, after which alcohol consumption diminished in the United States for the remainder of the century. According to W. J. Rorabaugh, the underlying reason for the "robust drinking" of the early nineteenth century was the unprecedented series of changes that occurred between 1790 and 1830 and, presumably, the increased stresses associated with these changes.[48] These included the development of the new, independent republic, industrialization in both the urban and rural areas, and increased immigration. Rorabaugh noted that during this time "almost every aspect of American life underwent alteration, in many cases startling upheaval...and...those groups most severely affected by change were also the groups most given to heavy drinking."[49]

Ill health was rampant in the cities in the early part of the nineteenth century. Epidemics of yellow fever, typhoid, and other diseases raged, their causes as yet unknown. City life seemed to contribute directly to ill health. There were frequent complaints of dyspepsia (a catch-all term for stomach pains, upsets, and other disorders). The general quality of medical care was poor.

When yellow fever appeared in areas where few people had acquired an immunity, the mortality rate was very high, often reaching fifty percent. The worst epidemic of yellow fever in North America occurred in 1793, in Philadelphia.[50] Despite the universal observation that yellow fever and mosquitoes came together, more than 100 years elapsed before the interrelationship was clearly understood. Fortunately, recovery from yellow fever is followed by lasting immunity. Today, this disease is contained largely through the control of mosquitoes and by immunization of persons at risk for exposure to the virus.

Despite the controversial nature of many of Dr. Benjamin Rush's treatments, his efforts to bring about improvements in public health during the colonial and early years of the Republic were laudable. But, unfortunately, they often have gone unrecognized. Between 1800 and 1850, while the United States expanded greatly in size and population, public health activities remained essentially stationary. This stalemate can be attributed to the many other pressing priorities which faced the new Republic during this period of rapid change. Meanwhile, threats to public health and welfare and the resultant incidence of disease were escalating. There were many, often recurrent epidemics, especially of smallpox, yellow fever, cholera, typhoid, and typhus. Definite epidemiological data relating to this era are limited. However, it is known that in Massachusetts in 1850 smallpox, scarlet fever, typhoid, and tuberculosis were still leading causes of death, and the infant mortality rate was about 200 per 1,000 live births. In fact, at this time, the average life expectancy in Boston and most of the other older cities in the United States was less than in London (long perceived as a city with serious public health concerns).[51] The above-mentioned diseases were poorly understood and the level and availability of appropriate medical care was inadequate. In addition, malnutrition contributed to the ease with which infections were contracted. "Fevers" were prevalent during this period, especially the ague or autumnal fevers of malaria (a mosquito-borne disease, which was endemic in the Ohio, Mississippi, and lower Missouri valleys.) In fact, malaria was so common that the intermittent fevers that accompanied it often were taken for granted.[52] Pneumonia was a constant threat, especially among infants, during this period. Endemic goiter, a non-contagious condition caused by a lack of iodine in the diet, was common during colonial times and the early years of the Republic. It was especially likely to occur in well-drained areas, away from the coast, where the iodine content of the soils was low and diets were lacking in seafood.

All of the men on the Lewis and Clark Expedition had been born during the late Colonial Period, except for George Shannon, the youngest, who was born in 1787, four years after the beginning of the new Republic. Thus, when these men joined the expedition in 1803, it is highly likely that their general nutritional status reflected many of the same dietary deficits which were typical during these contiguous periods (Table 1.2). However, some of these deficiencies would not become overtly expressed until later. Moreover, the selection process employed by the captains would have tended to favor those volunteers with the best health and nutritional histories.

Chapter 2
The Frontier Army Mess

Maintaining an army depends on a number of critical factors, including adequate clothing, weapons and ammunition, transportation, and food. An adequate food supply, however, is actually the top priority. Without it, the troops would perish. Sponsored by the United States government and led by United States Army officers Meriwether Lewis and William Clark, the expedition was clearly a special military undertaking. As such, the general army regulations would have been adhered to insofar as possible. Thus, the rules and practices for feeding the Corps of Discovery were basically those of the frontier army mess.

Aware of the pivotal role of food, on June 16, 1775, shortly after the onset of the Revolutionary War, the Second Continental Congress organized the Commissary General of Stores and Purchases. The purpose of the commissary was to furnish and supervise provisions for the Continental Army. On November 4, 1775, Congress established a uniform ration which remained in effect with relatively few changes for almost a century:

Per Day: 1 pound beef *or* ¾ pound pork *or* 1 pound salt fish; 1 pound bread *or* flour; 1 pint milk; 1 quart spruce beer *or* cider (or 9 gallons of molasses per company of 100 men per week)

Per Week: 3 pints peas *or* beans; ½ pint rice *or* 1 pint Indian meal; per 100 men/per week: 3 pounds candles, for the guards; 24 pounds soft soap *or* 8 pounds hard soap.

According to Barbara Luecke, these rations represented standards which, in practice, were rarely followed completely.[1]

During this period, "spruce beer" (in addition to fresh fruits and vegetables, when available) was commonly used in North America to prevent scurvy. Made from molasses, water, and spruce branches, spruce beer provided a good source of Vitamin C.[2]

By 1787, however, when the Congress of the new Republic passed legislation calling for a standing army of 840 men, the following ration was adopted: 1 pound bread *or* flour; 1 pound beef *or* ¾ pound of pork; 1 gill common rum. For every 100 rations, the following items were issued: 1 quart of salt, 2 quarts of vinegar, 2 pounds of soap and 1 pound of candles.[3] By 1802, the daily ration of a U.S. soldier was specified as "one and one quarter pounds of beef or three quarter pound of pork, 18 ounces of bread *or* flour, a gill of liquor, salt, vinegar, soap, and candles."[4]

Thus, beginning in 1787, soldiers were not lacking with respect to meat, bread and other cereal products, or leguminous vegetables. But, at this time, milk was omitted from the ration, and its lack lowered calcium and riboflavin intake considerably. Also, spruce beer (or molasses, from which to make it) was no longer supplied. Soldiers at army posts could obtain vitamin C from the fruits and vegetables found in the garrisons' gardens and orchards, but soldiers on the move did not have this advantage. Thus, they were at special risk for developing scurvy from a lack of vitamin C, as well as other dietary deficiencies.

The army ration did not change much between the American Revolution and the Civil War. Thus, by current nutritional standards (Table 1.1), the average officer, soldier, or camp follower, or any other person employed by the army and entitled to rations during this period (1775-1865) was consuming a diet that had numerous nutritional deficits. (The adequacy of the expedition's diet is assessed in detail in Chapter 6.)

In addition to the nutritional lacks of the rations themselves, there was the added problem caused by failures in delivery of provisions, or their substandard quality, for a variety of reasons. As early as May 1776, General George Washington was complaining that the lack of foodstuffs supplied to his troops was making it necessary for his men to forage for their own provisions.[5] Thus, living off the land by foraging was not unknown to Lewis and Clark, both of whom had been army officers prior to their embarking on the expedition. And, since they would be going into unknown territory, they realized that hunting, fishing, and gathering would be a daily necessity. In view of this situation, Lewis took special care in choosing men who were sturdy outdoorsmen, skilled at shooting and hunting, and able to endure hardships in the wilderness.[6]

Feeding the troops also was impeded by the various limitations reflecting the era itself, which influenced food preparation. At garrisons, the cooks lacked refrigeration, electricity, and other modern conveniences that are taken for granted today. Canning, first discovered in 1809 by Nicholas Appert, did not become widely used, in either military or civilian life, until the Civil War.[7] Efforts to preserve and store foods during the winter months were confined mainly to storage in root cellars. The amount of wood which each person received for both heating and cooking purposes was limited. Food was cooked over the fire indoors, both winter and summer, using as little wood as possible. Baking bread in the bakeshop further conserved wood.[8] Matches, such as are used today, were not invented until 1827. Prior to that date, fires were started with flint and steel. The use of such flints is mentioned in the Lewis and Clark journals. Kindling, or smaller sticks and wood shavings, was needed to light the fire, while medium-sized sticks and split wood were used to build and maintain it. In a fireplace, a pair of andirons was usually used as a support for logs, and the fire was then laid around them. However, in the absence of andirons and a fireplace (as was usually the case during the Lewis and Clark Expedition), a bonfire could be built, using iron or green wood spits. These spits spanned the fire between the crooks of two green sapling tree branches, sunk in the ground on either side of the fire. Next, meat or fish was "splinted" with skewers, which could then be fastened to the spit. Although the ideal type of wood for cooking in this manner is a hardwood, such as oak,[9] the frontier army (and, undoubtedly, the Corps of Discovery) tended to use any type of wood that was available.

Food preparation took place while the fire was burning down. The item baked or cooked determined the specific vessel needed to prepare a given type of food. The Lewis and Clark party used iron kettles and very likely spits also. While they may have had crude fireplaces at Fort Clatsop, most of their cooking was done using bonfires outdoors. An iron rod could then be used as a spit, or as a means of supporting a cord to which food (usually meat) was tied and suspended over the fire.

There are five methods that were commonly utilized in fireplace or open-fire cooking: roasting, boiling, baking, toasting, and broiling. The two most common methods used were roasting and boiling. The most simple roasting method was to truss the meat with a length of cord, tying it like a package. The other end of the cord was then tied to a hook or nail in the fireplace, allowing the meat to hang vertically in front of the fire. The cook would prod the cord with a fork, winding and unwinding it so that the meat would spin. A dripping pan was placed below the meat to catch the juices. Juices were then used to baste the meat and/or to make gravy.[10]

For boiling food, the fireplace generally had a crane attached to one of its side walls. Hangers could be attached to the crane to support large kettles and pots. These pot-hangers could be raised and lowered to adjust the cooking time of the food being prepared. Boiling consisted of placing meat in the kettle, covering it with water and gradually heating the contents. Boiling was continued until the food was done, with water replenished as needed.[11] Baking could also be done in the fireplace, utilizing the heat of the fireplace floor. The floor was large enough to hold various pots and kettles. Of these, the Dutch oven was generally used for daily baking. After pre-heating the oven, the cook placed the food in the oven in a container which was covered with a lid. The container was never placed directly on the oven floor, but rather on a trivet in the oven to prevent burning.[12]

Griddles were commonly used. The griddle was hung in the fireplace and was used to bake biscuits, griddle cakes, muffins, crumpets, scones, and pancakes. During the expedition, York (William Clark's servant) undoubtedly used a griddle to fry biscuit and other bread products. He could have hung the griddle by its wire handle from the overhead spit, or placed the griddle directly on the burning embers. In some cases, a long handled skillet or a spider (a skillet with feet) was used, with the griddle placed directly over the coals of the fireplace[13] or, possibly, over the embers of a bonfire.

During this period, bread and soup were the mainstays of the soldier's diet. Meats were generally boiled with a view to making soup.[14] After bread and soup, beans were probably the most commonly consumed food in the military, the exact variety depending on the geographical area of the post from which they were obtained. Beans were a good staple item, since they are easy to store and can be kept for long periods of time in a dry storage space. Dried peas also were frequently used for the same reasons.

The army breads tended to be unleavened. According to Luecke, no army-regulated recipe for yeast has been found.[15] Moreover, sodium bicarbonate as a leavening agent did not become available until around the late 1830s;[16] baking powder became commercially available in 1856.[17] Thus, most of the breads consumed by the military during this era, such as the popular corn breads, likely were unleavened.

As stated earlier, it was expected that the captains would follow general army regulations as much as possible with respect to feeding the members of the expedition. However, even at Camp Dubois, the corps was operating under special circumstances. In these cases, the captains made their own rules. For example, that winter, Clark engaged some of the men in making sugar (presumably from molasses) and, as a reward, gave these men an additional ration of whiskey.

Following general army guidelines, Lewis began his preparations for the anticipated trip during the spring and early summer of 1803. One of the first things he accomplished while in Philadelphia was the purchase of 193 pounds of "portable soup" for the party (see Chapter 3). But, even as he made these preparations, Lewis was aware that, on this exploratory mission into uncharted territory, the group would usually be far from established forts or garrisons, where the usual regulations probably would not apply. In these cases, the regulations would have to be altered on an *ad hoc* basis. He knew that his men would not usually have access to the meals and rations customarily consumed by army personnel occupying that "archipelago" of garrisons strung along the western frontier at the turn of the nineteenth century.[18] However, he did make plans to take along provisions of the type customarily consumed by the army at that time. But planning was difficult, particularly because there were still so many unknowns. Critical unknown factors included the final size of the party and both the length and duration of the trip.

The captains realized that, in any event, lack of space on the boats would prevent taking along sufficient consumable dry goods to last the entire trip. But they decided to take along as much as they could. Table 5.1 provides a listing of the provisions which Lewis and Clark prepared shortly before the corps's departure from Wood River on May 14, 1804. In a notation made following this list, Captain Clark referred to these provisions as sufficient for the party for forty days (presumably in case of an emergency).[19] In practice, however, they were used sparingly throughout the trip west.

It was customary for traders and explorers during this era to bring along jerky and pemmican on their journeys. These concentrated foods were resistant to spoilage and were compact and nutritious. In fact, pemmican represented an almost perfect food for travelers, particularly if it contained berries, which it usually did. The word *pemmican* comes from the Cree Indian word *pimikân*. The Cree Indians (one of the subarctic Indian tribes who live in Canada and Montana) perhaps were among the first Indians to make this food. It tended to be made by those Indians who lived on the prairies south of the forest belt, where the buffalo provided an abundant supply of meat and fat.[20] Pemmican was widely used by these tribes for bartering with the traders and early pioneers.

President Jefferson and Meriwether Lewis had read Alexander Mackenzie's account of his voyage to the Pacific while Lewis was vacationing at Monticello during the summer of 1802.[21] Therefore, they obviously were aware that it was pemmican that had saved the Mackenzie party from starvation during this long journey. Yet neither pemmican nor jerky, one of its key ingredients, is listed as one of the provisions to be taken along on the Lewis and Clark Expedition (Table 5.1). However, the journals indicate that, once underway, the men did proceed to make jerky, and, later, pemmican. As early as June 5, the corps was making jerky by sun-drying meat which the hunters had killed. There are subsequent references to "jerking" meat at intervals throughout the trip. Then, going up the Missouri on June 12, both of the captains noted that the party had bought 300 pounds of "voyager's grease" from some fur traders coming downstream. "Voyager's grease" was a mixture of buffalo grease and tallow,[22] commonly used as a base material to which dried and pounded meat and cherries or berries were added for the making of pemmican. On June 13, 1805, Captain Clark wrote, "The Hunters killed 3 Buffalow the most of all the meat I had dried for to make Pemitigon [pemmican]."

From the onset, Captain Lewis had known that the greatest share of food would have to come, not from their carefully packed provisions, but "off the land," mainly by hunting and foraging. Thus, Lewis also was keenly aware of the need for adequate ammunition and weapons for the expedition, not only for self-defense, but for the procurement of game en route. That he also expected the men to fish is evidenced by his purchase of fish hooks and fish gigs as part of the supplies. The high priority placed on firearms and ammunition is not surprising, and it is evidenced by Lewis's relatively early visit to the U.S. Army's arsenal at Harpers Ferry, in mid-March, 1803. Here, he selected weapons ranging from knives and tomahawks to rifles, flints, and gunpowder, packed in waterproof lead canisters. At Harpers Ferry, he also got fifteen muzzle-loading flintlock, long-barreled rifles, which proved to be critical for the corps's food supply and self-defense.

One very important advantage enjoyed by the Lewis and Clark Expedition while wintering at Camp Dubois (December 1803-May 1804) was that the party was able to obtain provisions and other supplies periodically through the Commissary of Subsistence at nearby St. Louis. There were many contractors in the area who supplied the upper Mississippi River posts at that time, as well as the Lewis and Clark party. In this way, the corps was able to obtain food for its immediate use, as well as add to supplies obtained earlier as they prepared for the upcoming voyage. At the point of departure, the expedition consisted of about fifty people, including *engagés*.

Chapter 3
Medical Aspects of the Expedition

People who are on expeditions of any kind usually are on the move, often under adverse conditions and without the usual supports and infrastructures which make for a dependable food supply. Also, they tend not to remain long enough in any one place to become familiar enough with the ecosystem to determine the most effective ways and means of obtaining food there. Consequently, they often are faced with dietary scarcities.

For these reasons, historically, malnutrition has been an almost constant condition of soldiers. One facet of this condition can be under-nutrition, or insufficient food. This condition produces debilitating effects such as fatigue and lack of energy, which impede performance. In addition, malnutrition can produce more specific non-contagious conditions which stem from one or more dietary lacks. Among these, perhaps the most common has been scurvy, caused by a lack of vitamin C, found mainly in fresh fruits and vegetables. In addition, such a compromised nutritional status predisposes individuals to the development of many diseases, both chronic and acute, from which soldiers commonly have suffered (see Chapter 6).

The Lewis and Clark Expedition was no exception. The party experienced the usual diseases contracted by the military during the Revolutionary War and the War of 1812. These included malaria, dysentery, diarrhea, rheumatism, respiratory diseases (e.g., pneumonia), ophthalmia, venereal disease, and other maladies. During the War of 1812, "...the great scourges were the intestinal and the respiratory infections,"[1] to which the Lewis and Clark party also fell prey. At Fort Clatsop, for example, the men suffered from an epidemic of colds and fevers, influenza-like conditions similar to those that affected American soldiers in World War I. It is highly likely that most of the members of the Lewis and Clark party also had a chronic malarial condition, with intermittent bouts of ague. But the only episode that was specifically recorded and described was by Lewis, regarding himself, in September 1803.

Soldiers of this era were vulnerable to disease for many reasons. Both the quality and quantity of food were usually low. During the Revolutionary War, food supplies were even shorter than medical supplies.[2] It was understood that soldiers would augment their food supplies by foraging for food. In addition, they generally experienced squalid living conditions and exposure to the elements. Clothing often was inadequate or inappropriate for conditions, and the sanitation level was low. Housing usually was primitive and drinking water frequently inadequate and/or contaminated. Infectious diseases were much more frequent than chronic diseases, mainly because most of the soldiers were young and had not yet developed the chronic diseases commonly associated with middle to old age. However, despite their youth, they suffered from such conditions as constipation from dehydration and/or lack of dietary fiber, dyspepsia, rheumatism, and various injuries associated with their physically demanding activities.

Medical practitioners of this period held many false beliefs that are shocking today. This period preceded, of course, the development of the germ theory of disease by Louis

Pasteur in the early 1860s and the development of Robert Koch's postulates of disease in the 1870s. These men effected revolutionary advances, both in the understanding of the microbiological causes of infectious diseases and in their treatment. But, at this time, the relationship between uncleanliness and sepsis was not yet known.[3]

In the early 1800s, fevers were categorized as separate entities, not manifestations of many illnesses. Body temperatures were determined by touching and observing the patient, rather than by using a thermometer, since body thermometers were not developed until 1870. Powders and other preparations containing Peruvian bark, obtained from South America, were used in the treatment of all sorts of fevers, but mainly for the ague, or "autumnal fevers," a recurrent symptom of malaria. Although Peruvian bark had a general ability to lower fevers, it also contained a specific, active ingredient that attacked the causative organism itself, a protozoan called Plasmodium. This active substance was quinine, first extracted from Peruvian bark in 1845.

Purging, vomiting, sweating, and bleeding were widely accepted curative procedures. The prevailing belief was that fevers were the result of the morbid condition of the blood vessels and that bleeding assisted sweating, vomiting, and diarrhea as nature's ways of depleting the body of its morbid elements. Certain medicines were used specifically to induce sweating (diaphoretics) or vomiting (emetics). Purging was brought about by the use of laxatives, or purgatives. Blood-letting was used for many different illnesses, including malaria. Its advocates believed that the blood was the site of the disease, thus it should be depleted. Blood-letting was such a common practice that the lancet became the symbol of the physician just before and during the time of the Lewis and Clark Expedition.

Unfortunately, bleeding often did more harm than good. Many people became so depleted of blood that they were seriously weakened. George Washington, for example, during his final illness, may have been bled too much. His doctor removed one gallon and a pint of blood within twenty-four hours. However, since he already suffered from two serious conditions (septic sore throat and pneumonia), he probably would have died anyway. These diseases were great killers prior to the comparatively recent advent of antibiotics. A serious drawback for physicians at that time was that they did not yet know the normal volume of blood in the human adult body, nor whether they were bleeding patients who already were anemic.

The most famous and vocal proponent of blood-letting in the early 1800s was Dr. Benjamin Rush, of Philadelphia, who became one of Captain Lewis's tutors during his preparations for the expedition. Blood-letting had ancient origins, preceding Hippocrates and other early men of medicine. It continued to be used through the centuries until long after Lewis and Clark's time, and remained a common medical treatment up to the time of the Civil War. However, its use had begun to decline in America after 1830, not too long after Dr. Benjamin Rush's death in 1813.[4] Dr. Eldon Chuinard recalled that it was still being used occasionally during the late 1930s, while he was serving as an intern, for the treatment of hypertension.[5]

On February 28, 1803, President Jefferson wrote to Dr. Rush asking him to help Lewis prepare for the journey.[6] The president had sought out Dr. Rush because he was the most eminent physician in the United States, and had been since Colonial times. According to Dr. Chuinard, "His energy and unfailing readiness to utter and write opinions on all things medical and political made him the most widely known and controversial physician of the day, if not the most highly regarded by some of his professional colleagues.[7]

Meriwether Lewis came to Dr. Rush for medical instruction on May 17, 1803. Rush is quoted by David Freeman Hawke as having said, "That officer...will best perform his duty to his men, who obliges them to take the most care of their health."[8] Possessing this conviction, Dr. Rush probably began by reiterating the high points of a publication that he had written in 1777 entitled, "Directions for Preserving the Health of Soldiers, Addressed to the Officers of the Army of the United States."[9] Following is a summary of its five main points:

1. Dress should be of flannel instead of linen, since flannel is less disposed to form miasmata, which produces fevers.
2. Diet should consist chiefly of vegetables, well cooked. Spoiled meats and flour should be avoided. Rum was a part of army diet, but Rush was against its overuse, recommending a mixture of vinegar and water instead.
3. Personal cleanliness was important, including the frequent washing of the body, clothing, eating utensils, and bedding. Hair was to be worn short on the neck, and combed frequently. Hands and face were to be washed daily, and the body was to be bathed at least three times a week.
4. Camps must be kept clean, moved frequently, and located away from the "effluvia" of swampy places.
5. Rush recognized the age-old problem of army and civilian personnel, that idleness was the bane of everyone, and that a disciplined attention to duty was necessary.

He then may have gone on to advocate the popular treatments of the day, including fasting and diluting drinks for the prevention of fever, the promotion of sweating, vomiting, diuresis, and purging, using Rush's patented pills, known as "Rush's pills" or "Thunderclappers," for almost any ailment. The latter was a mixture of calomel (mercurous chloride) and jalap (a tuberous root grown in Mexico), both of which have cathartic attributes. Undoubtedly, Rush also instructed him to use calomel in the treatment of syphilis as well, even though both Lewis and Clark had already become familiar with this treatment during their tenure as army officers. Above all, he would have stressed the use of blood-letting for many medical problems.

From the perspective of today's medical knowledge, there were a number of serious errors in Dr. Rush's thinking and in the thinking of other practitioners of this era. Even at that time, many of his ideas were controversial. Yet much of his advice was good. Indeed, in some instances, Dr. Rush turned out to be right, even though for the wrong reasons. His advice for the treatment of malaria is a prime example. Mosquitoes were not yet identified as a causative factor in malaria in the time of Lewis and Clark, but by that time it had been noted that it seemed to occur near wetlands and decomposing material. Therefore, it was hypothesized that such places gave off "miasmata," "effluvia," and/or "exhalations," all of which were harmful to a person when inhaled. The apparent relationship of the disease to stagnant water and the desirability of fresh air led Dr. Rush to recommend that swamps be drained and the soldiers kept on the move. It is now well known that the lessened incidence of malaria under the above circumstances was due to fewer mosquitoes in drained areas. And keeping soldiers on the move was desirable because it allowed them to leave dirty, poorly ventilated, germ-laden quarters behind, thus preventing constant re-infection.

Dr. Rush provided his most valuable assistance to the expedition by giving Lewis advice on what medicines and medical supplies he believed should be purchased for the undertaking (Table 3.1). Lewis obtained these items from the drug firm of Gillaspay &

Strong of Philadelphia, through Israel Wheelen, purveyor of the Schuylkill arsenal in Philadelphia, and receipted for them himself. The list may reflect the advice of several medical contacts in Philadelphia but most particularly that of Dr. Rush. It is of interest that the catalog of medicine for the army in 1776 was very similar to the items that Lewis purchased for the trip.[10]

It is thought that the captains bought more medicines and medical supplies later, before leaving Camp Dubois, from Dr. Saugrain of St. Louis. For example, considering the frequency with which laudanum was used for pain, they would have needed much more than four ounces for the entire trip. It is not surprising that Lewis bought a generous supply (fifty dozen) of "Bilious pills," since they had been originally formulated by Dr. Rush himself. He strongly advocated taking them for many maladies, including constipation. They contained calomel and jalap, both potent cathartics.

The large amount of Peruvian bark powder purchased for the journey indicates that the captains expected fevers to be a major health concern, particularly the recurrent "ague" of malaria. They were very much aware that malaria was endemic in the Ohio, Mississippi,

Table 3.1–Bill of Gillaspay & Strong for Medicine*

Israel Wheelen Purveyor Bought of Gillaspay & Strong the following articles for the use of M. Lewis Esquire on his tour up the Mississippi River, and supplied by his Order: -Viz.

15 lb.	Pulv.	Cort. Peru		$30.00	4 oz.	Laudanum		.50
½ lb.	"	Jalap		.67	2 lb.	Ung. Basilic Flav.	.50	1.00
½ lb.	"	Rhei [Rhubarb]		1.00	1 lb. " [...] Calimin.		.50	.50
4 oz.	"	Ipecacuan		1.25	1 lb. " Epipastric			1.00
2 lb.	"	Cream. Tart.		.67	1 lb. " Mercuriale			1.25
2 oz.	Gum	Camphor		.40	1	Emplast. Diach. S.		.50
1 lb.	"	Assafoetid.		1.00	1	Set Pocket Insts. small		9.50
½ lb.	"	Opii Turk. opt.		2.50	1	" Teeth " "		2.25
¼ lb.	"	Tragacanth		.37	1	Clyster Syringe		2.75
6 lb.	Sal	Glauber	.10	.60	4	Penis do.		1.00
2 lb.	"	Nitri	.33½	.67	3	Best Lancets	.80	2.40
2 lb.	Copperas			.10	1	Tourniquet		3.50
6 oz.	Sacchar.Satur.opt.			.37	2 oz.	Patent Lint		.25
4 oz.	Calomel			.75	50 doz. Bilious Pills to Order			
1 oz.	Tartar Emetic			.10		of Dr. Rush	.10	5.00
4 oz.	Vitriol Alb.			.12	6 Tin Canisters		.25	1.50
½ lb.	Rad. Columbo			1.00	3 8 oz. Gd. Stopd. bottles			1.20
¼ lb.	Elix. Vitriol			.25	5 4 oz. Tinctures do			1.85
¼ lb.	Ess. Menth. pip.			.50	6 4 oz. Salt Mo.			2.22
¼ lb.	Bals. Copaiboe			.37	1 Walnut Chest			4.50
¼ lb.	" Traumat.			.50	1 Pine do.			1.20
2 oz.	Magnesia			.20		Porterage		.30
¼ lb.	Indian Ink			1.50	**Total**			**$90.69**
2 oz.	Gum Elastic			.37				
2 oz.	Nutmegs			.75				
2 oz.	Cloves			.31				
4 oz.	Cinnamon			.20				
	Subtotal			**$46.52**		*Phila. May 26, 1803*		

* "Do" is the abbreviation for "ditto." Jackson, 1962: 80-81.

and lower Missouri valleys during this time. And, since they would be following rivers much of the time, they probably expected to continue to encounter this medical problem as they went westward. Because malaria was so prevalent in the area from which the men had been recruited, it is surprising that the journals never explicitly refer to any of the party suffering from "ague," except for Lewis's bout in September 1803. Many must have had it, but it probably was regarded as too common to mention.

Sal nitri or saltpeter was used as a diuretic and diaphoretic for fevers and probably gonorrhea. Opii Turk was probably used as an alternative to laudanum. Obtained by drying the milk of the poppy, it also contained opium. Lewis purchased a good supply of ingredients with which to make "eye wash," including white vitriol (zinc sulfate) and sugar of lead, or lead acetate (cited on the list as "Sacchar.Satur.opt"). These were in high demand, since many of the men developed sore eyes en route. These preparations also proved to be a valuable diplomatic tool in the party's relationship with the Indians, particularly the Nez Perce, on the way back. In fact, the Indians which the corps met throughout the expedition frequently had chronic eye problems, caused by one or more of the following: gonorrhea (gonococcal conjunctivitis in the newborn), syphilis, myopia, trachoma, and various purulent infections. In addition, certain nutrient deficiencies cause eye problems, from which both the Indians and the Lewis and Clark party suffered (e.g., lack of vitamin C, vitamin A, and others.)

The captains had lancets and a tourniquet for bleeding and plenty of medicine for purging, but a surprisingly low supply of emetics. They took along a small amount of ipecacuan (ipecac), a traditional component of home health kits, for the induction of vomiting. But it would appear from their lack of mention in the journals that emetics were seldom used on the expedition.

Some of the items on the list were used in decoctions and salves, to improve the flavor and aroma. Others were plasters or ointments used for ameliorative purposes in ointments, to be applied on cuts, abrasions, and blisters.[11]

The inclusion of four penis syringes indicated that the men expected gonorrhea to be one of their medical problems. These articles were used for the standard urethral irrigations of the day (probably using solutions of Saccharum saturni and the balsam of copaiba). The clyster syringe was to be used for enemas, but from the journal entries one concludes that the men rarely used that treatment for constipation. They apparently preferred Rush's pills. In addition to these, they had several other drugs which had laxative effects: jalap, rhubarb, cream of tartar, Glauber's salts, calomel, and a magnesium preparation, probably magnesium sulfate (Epsom salts).

Captain Lewis also is known to have bought thirty gallons of "strong, Spt. wine" for $77.20, almost as much as was spent for medical supplies.[12] Probably intended to be part of the medical supplies, the wine had been obtained from a druggist in Philadelphia named D. Jackson.[13] An important purchase was made on Lewis's behalf by Israel Wheelen of "193 pounds of portable soup." It was contained in lead canisters and may have been either a dry powder or a thick liquid substance. It had been made by Francis Baillet, a Philadelphia cook, who presented a bill for the soup in the amount of $289.50 on May 30, 1803.[14] It probably was very similar to other portable soups used by armed forces of the time. Soup usually was made from meat (beef, mutton, or veal) which had been well-boiled. Then the liquid was separated from it, and when cold, the fat was removed. After salting to taste, it was boiled down to a paste, dried, and placed in closed containers of tin or glass. Before use, it was reconstituted with water and given to the sick. It could also be served to the rest of the party when food was scarce, usually with powdered rice, beans, peas, barley, or celery added.[15] Lewis specifically referred to the portable soup as being contained in canisters in his note of September 18, 1805. Later on, the used canisters were melted down to make bullets.

The soup was ready in plenty of time. Lewis receipted for it and took it with him overland to Pittsburgh, where he was to embark on the Ohio River. The portable soup proved to be a life-saver for the corps at various critical times during the expedition, serving as an alternative to pemmican. The Lewis and Clark Expedition long preceded the landmark work of Louis Pasteur and his germ theory of the 1860s and even the initial discovery of canning by Nicholas Appert, a French scientist, in 1809. These discoveries paved the way for the actual use of canning during the Civil War by the U.S. armed forces.

While in Philadelphia during much of May and the first week of June 1803, Lewis picked up three bushels of salt, as well as many other items to be used for the trip. His total expenditure for food and drugs amounted to $2,324, almost as much as had been granted him originally for the entire expedition.

Lewis may have briefly considered obtaining a physician to accompany the party on the expedition, but there are no indications in the journals that he seriously sought one. His failure to do so is understandable. First, since both Lewis and Clark had spent some time in the army as officers, they had learned and practiced currently accepted procedures for health care. Here, they had gained experience in venesection, or blood-letting, and many other techniques. And, growing up on the frontier, they undoubtedly had learned early how to set a broken bone or dislocated shoulder, remove an embedded bullet, and carry out basic first-aid procedures.

As captains, they were very aware that commanding officers of the era were considered directly responsible for the health of the men under them. And they probably felt they were as well-qualified to take on the challenge as the civilian doctors of the day, considering the small amount of preparation most practitioners underwent. Most doctors became trained through apprenticeships. Lewis and Clark's skills had been learned as part of their training as officers, then honed by caring for the soldiers under them. At the time of the American Revolution, there were only two medical schools in America, at the University of Philadelphia (organized in 1765), and in New York (begun in 1768). Licensure was slow in coming to the South and the new Republic. In fact, the first of such laws was not passed until 1817, in South Carolina, while the first board examination was held in Mississippi in 1819. Both of these events occurred well after the Lewis and Clark Expedition.

Lewis had an additional advantage in that he came from a medically oriented family. Both his brother, Reuben, and half-brother, John Marks, became medical doctors. His mother was an herbalist, a student of herbal medicine, and from her he had assimilated a sizeable store of practical medical knowledge. She was well known for miles around Locust Hill, the family estate near Charlottesville, Virginia, for riding miles on horseback to care for the sick. She taught Lewis how to make various decoctions, or "simples," which were herbal preparations made by steeping herbs in boiling water, to be used for sore eyes and other ailments.

Lewis had all of his medical supplies assembled and receipted by March 27, 1803. His other supplies were ready, and he had received all of his instructions. He then returned to Washington prior to his planned departure westward. Here, he spent several days conferring with President Jefferson, reviewing the final plans for the expedition before departing from Pittsburgh down the Ohio to the West on August 31, 1803.

One of the surprises in store for Lewis and Clark was the level of medical knowledge and practice already possessed by the Indians with whom the corps came in contact during the expedition. Their level of medical expertise at that time still is not widely known and appreciated and deserves to be both acknowledged and discussed.

By the time the colonists arrived, the Indians already were very knowledgeable regarding the medicinal uses of plant preparations for various health conditions. They had also developed skill in the treatment of fractures equal to that of the white man up to and during the time of Lewis and Clark.[16] They had independently developed such practices of the white man as splinting, traction, and immobilization, and were very knowledgeable about the healing time for various broken bones in the human body. According to Eric Stone, "Their skill in the care of wounds, fractures, and dislocations equalled, and in some respects, exceeded that of their white contemporary."[17] They also were skilled in treating burns, ulcers, and infections. Dr. Maurice Gordon has noted that "the American Indians handled their wounds, empyemas [pustular infections], fractures, and dislocations as well [as] if not better, than the 18th century white physicians. Their method of removing a retained placenta preceded the development of a similar method by the well-known German obstetrician Karl Credé (1819-1892), by a hundred years."[18]

When Sacagawea went into labor on February 11, 1805, at Fort Mandan, Captain Lewis attended her, his first (and presumably, his only) infant delivery. This was her first child, and, according to Lewis, "...her labor was tedious and the pain violent." He consulted with René Jessaume (a French trader who served as an interpreter for the Mandans), who had gained experience on the frontier in attending women during childbirth. He informed Lewis that he frequently administered a small portion of a rattle-snake tail, which, he assured Lewis, never failed to hasten the birth of the child. Fortuitously, Lewis had some of this material on hand, which he gave to Jessaume. The latter broke two rings of it into small pieces, mixed it with a small quantity of water, and administered it to Sacagawea. Within ten minutes, she "brought forth" at 5 p.m. that afternoon.[19] Whether the pulverized rings of the rattlesnake actually hastened the delivery has been the subject of much controversy among health professionals. Captain Lewis himself was dubious as to its merits. However, rattlesnake venom is known to contain a neurotoxin, which, in small quantities, can serve as a muscle relaxant. And it is conceivable that any venom which is not discharged through the fangs would, like other waste products, pass out of the snake's body through a cavity called a cloaca. Here, waste material collects, and is eliminated through a vent that is directly adjacent to the rattler's tail.[20] Thus, some of the neurotoxin conceivably could become absorbed by the rattles, which then could serve as a muscle relaxant if ingested.

The Indians had a good understanding of basic physiological processes, such as sweating, constipation, emesis, menstruation, and parturition. The journals of Lewis and Clark describe how Captain Clark used the "Indian sweat" to bring about a miraculous cure on the return journey. Constipation was treated with herbs having purging properties; horns and animal bladders were used to administer enemas. The Indians also were astute enough to keep the sick isolated in their own lodges, thus avoiding "hospital gangrene," the scourge of military hospitals of that day. Also, by keeping "on the move," the Indians kept contagion to a minimum (see Chapter 7).[21]

It is of interest that the Indian people also were using the "standbys" of the white man during this period—blood-letting, purging, sweating, and vomiting—for the general treatment of diseases. And they followed the universally recognized health practices of heat, poulticing, rest, and cleanliness. Many tribes advocated daily bathing.[22]

From a medical point of view, the real disadvantage that the Native Americans of this era suffered was lack of immunity and resistance to the diseases being brought to this continent by the white man, principally malaria and smallpox. Although the white population was also vulnerable to these diseases, many of these newcomers had at least partial immunity to some of them because of prior exposure.[23]

Chapter 4
Preparing for the Expedition

Approximately sixteen months (January 1803-May 1804) were spent in preparation for the expedition, beginning with the early discussions of President Thomas Jefferson and Captain Meriwether Lewis, the latter's journey down the Ohio picking up recruits and bringing William Clark on board at Clarksville, followed by the corps's wintering at Camp Dubois on the Wood River, across the Mississippi from St. Louis.

President Jefferson, following authorization by Congress in January 1803, had provided the broad objectives for the expedition. Now it was up to Lewis to implement them. So Lewis began to make plans and decisions. As with all explorations, there were many unknowns, which made planning an extremely open-ended and difficult process.

Lewis and Jefferson had roughly outlined some of the more obvious needs early in 1803, during January, February, and early March. They needed men with specific skills, boats for transportation, guns, ammunition, non-perishable food, cooking utensils, and tools. But Jefferson also wanted careful observations made of flora and fauna, both general and scientific, as the party moved westward into unknown territory. That spring, in preparation for the more scientific aspects of the trip, the President sent Captain Lewis to Lancaster, Pennsylvania, for instruction in celestial observations, then to the University of Pennsylvania at Philadelphia. There, four scientists tutored him in describing and preserving botanical specimens and in determining latitude and longitude. Lewis also was given lessons on fossils. For medical advice, he was counseled by Dr. Benjamin Rush, the nation's preeminent physician of that time.

Soon, Lewis began making many lists of the various things that would be needed for the journey and then set out to acquire them. By mid-June, the army had begun transporting 3,500 pounds of supplies to the Ohio River, in preparation for the trip westward to St. Louis. Included were the firearms, other weapons, and ammunition purchased earlier from the arsenal in Harpers Ferry.

Captain Lewis's early awareness of the need for adequate food supplies is demonstrated by his inclusion of 193 pounds of "portable soup." This thick paste, made by boiling down beef, eggs, and vegetables, was to be used if no other food was available on the trail. As he focused on food purchases, Lewis obviously recognized that his food needs were twofold: first, provisions for the expedition, and, second, the more immediate needs of the trip down the Ohio to St. Louis. Primarily, he needed staples that would not spoil readily, such as flour, meal, and salt pork. These were loaded at Pittsburgh, along with the other supplies. Since the planned expedition was a "military operation" under the auspices of the United States Government, Lewis, of course, was strongly guided by the current regulations and procedures of the United States Army regarding the food rations and related items supplied to military personnel at that time.

Lewis knew that, going down the Ohio, he would be in known, albeit increasingly frontier, territory. So he expected to be able to pick up various items of food along the way from farmers and merchants. But, because procuring them would be unpredictable and time-consuming, he realized that the group would still need to rely mainly on hunting to augment its food supply. This meant that, ideally, all of the men in the party should be skilled at hunting. In fact, Captain Lewis himself had been chosen by President Jefferson to serve as commanding officer of this group in part because he was "habituated to the hunting life."[1]

At this point, Lewis considered St. Louis to be a mere stopping point, a place from which to launch the expedition up the Missouri River toward Mandan country. By 1803, there had been enough traffic up and down the river by fur traders and others that the general aspects of the Missouri River were quite well known. Unfortunately, Lewis could not foresee the delays that were about to slow things up considerably. He still hoped (unrealistically, as it turned out) to arrive at St. Louis early enough in the summer for the party to proceed to Mandan, remain there briefly, then proceed westward. He anticipated that they would reach the coast before fall, and remain there for the winter.

Finally, on August 30, 1803, Lewis, with "a party of 11 hands 7 of which are soldiers, a pilot and three young men,"[2] left Pittsburgh in a 55-foot keelboat and a pirogue on their way down the Ohio River (Figure 4.1). The water level by now was very low. In order to keep the keelboat as high in the water as possible, Lewis had decided to lighten its load by purchasing the smaller boat to carry some of the goods. Later, at Wheeling, he purchased another pirogue to carry some goods that had been shipped overland from Pittsburgh.

At Wheeling, Lewis decided to give the men a day's rest "and let them wash their clothes and exchange their flour for bread, or bake their bread in a better manner than they had the means while traveling...," referring to the practice of having their bread prepared at a bakery. After the men got their bread, the group set out on September 10. On September 11, Lewis described the first example of "food getting" on the expedition, and, interestingly, not by the men. That day, some squirrels were migrating across the Ohio, and Seaman, Lewis's Newfoundland, began barking at them. Lewis allowed him to swim out to the squirrel, which the dog killed and brought back to Lewis. He then sent Seaman back for more. The squirrels were fat, and when fried, Lewis found them "a plesent food."

Squirrel meat proved to be such a welcome addition to their diets, that, on September 14, Captain Lewis wrote that he caught several more of these animals "by means of my dog—." On September 16, he went on shore and obtained some more squirrels with his gun.

On September 12, Lewis wrote that, in the evening, he had bought "some corn and pittatoes for my men" from a Yankee farmer, giving him in exchange a few pounds of lead. This was the first of many instances in which the party obtained food from people they encountered en route.

On September 17, Lewis reported that "my biscuit was much injured" from the rain of the 15th: "I had it picked and put up in these baggs [of oilcloth]—this work kept [me] so busy that I ate nothing until after dark, being determined to have everything in readiness for a early start in the morning...." Both his English and southern colonial background are evident in Lewis's referring to this bread product (biscuits) in the singular, rather than the plural form.[3] This "biscuit" was either a crisp, dry bread baked in thin, hard flat cakes, or a cracker. In either form, this type of bread product was commonly used by soldiers, sailors (who called it hardtack), and explorers, all of whom needed non-perishable food. Because of its dryness and the absence of shortening or a leavening agent it had high keeping qualities.

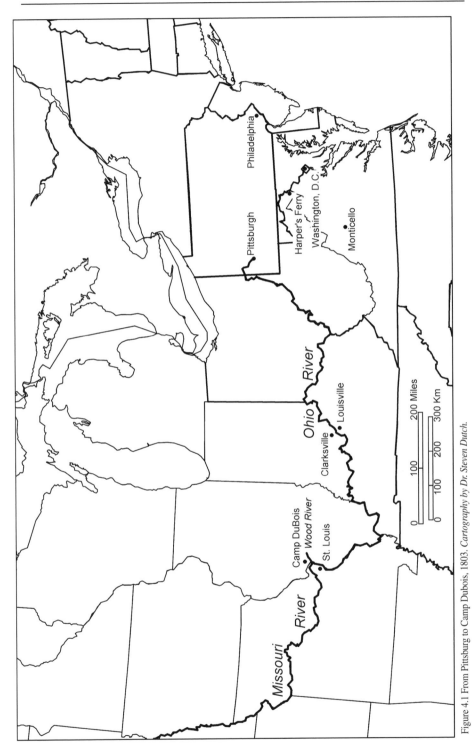

Figure 4.1 From Pittsburg to Camp Dubois, 1803. *Cartography by Dr. Steven Dutch.*

On October 3, Lewis wrote President Jefferson a letter in which he indicated that, because of several delays, he would be building a winter camp at St. Louis, rather than going further up the Missouri. Surprisingly, Jefferson was happy with Lewis's decision because he himself had recently decided that he wanted Lewis to spend the winter in St. Louis rather than upstream somewhere. Jefferson wanted him to gather information regarding some important political events which might be occurring there. Also, considering the lateness of the season, it would be wiser for the expedition to be at St. Louis, where it could draw its rations from nearby United States Army commissaries on the Mississippi, rather than depleting its stores intended for the planned journey up river. Jefferson obviously recognized the overriding importance of food as a critical factor in the success of the expedition.

After a few months of planning, Meriwether Lewis realized that he would need help in leading the expedition. Jefferson had previously discussed the wisdom of adding another officer to assist Lewis and approved of it in concept. Accordingly, on June 19, 1803, Lewis had written his friend Captain William Clark, who earlier had been his army superior, to share the leadership of this formidable undertaking. He accepted, and on October 15, when Lewis and his men reached Clarksville, in Indiana Territory, William Clark joined the party.

The news had spread that men were needed for the expedition, and numerous young men came from up and down the Ohio hoping to be selected. Together, Lewis and Clark proceeded to evaluate them, looking for such qualities as general hardiness, marksmanship and hunting skills, physical strength, good character, and ability to withstand a long journey under potentially trying conditions. The captains continued with their selections as they descended the Ohio.

On November 11, they arrived at Fort Massac, about thirty-five miles upstream from the junction of the Ohio and the Mississippi. Here, Lewis engaged George Drewyer (Drouillard) in the public service as an Indian interpreter and contracted to pay him "25 dollars pr. month for his services."[4] The son of a French Canadian father and a Shawnee mother, Drouillard was a skilled frontiersman, hunter/trapper, and scout.

On November 13, the expedition set off about 5 p.m. from Fort Massac. That evening, Lewis was seized with a violent ague, which continued about four hours. He was having an attack of malaria.

On November 16, a little below the junction of the Ohio and the Mississippi, the men, having crossed to the western side, caught a huge catfish weighing 128 pounds. It was probably a blue catfish, which could have weighed 150 pounds or more.[5] Lewis noted that he and Clark had been accustomed to seeing catfish only thirty to sixty pounds in weight. But, despite their obvious interest in this fish, there is no record of their having actually eaten it.

On November 20, as the expedition headed out into the Mississippi, then turned upstream toward Cape Girardeau, they were assailed by the awesome power of that river. This experience, coupled with the river's tedious "bends," convinced the captains that they would need more pairs of hands as they continued upriver.

On November 22, Lewis reported that they "set out at ½ after 6 a.m....saw some Heth hens or grows—one of my men went on shore and killed one of them, of which we made some soup for my friend Capt. Clark, who has been indisposed since the 16th ...."

On November 23, the party landed at Cape Girardeau, where Louis Lorimer was the commandant. On the 24th, they proceeded northward, arriving at Horse Island the evening of the 27th. On the 28th, they set out from the lower point of Horse Island opposite the mouth of Kaskaskies [Kaskaskia] River, passing its mouth at half past 8 o'clock. Here, Lewis left Captain Clark in charge of the boat, while he remained at Kaskaskia to make astronomical observations. Lewis left Kaskaskia on December 5, traveling up the Illinois bank by horseback. He arrived at the village of Cahokia, almost directly across from St. Louis, on December 7. The next day, Lewis crossed the river to St. Louis along with Nicholas Jarrot (a Cahokia fur trader and interpreter) to meet the Spanish commandant at St. Louis, Colonel Carlos Dehault Delassus. Now the Spanish lieutenant governor of Upper Louisiana, Delassus denied Lewis permission to go up the Missouri until the transfer of sovereignty had taken place. Lewis calmly accepted his decision; it was too late in the season to go on anyway. Besides, Lewis needed to be near St. Louis to purchase more supplies before embarking on the expedition. After all, only 3,500 pounds of provisions had been loaded at Pittsburgh and he now had a larger party than he had then anticipated. More men meant that more food and supplies would be needed.

Nicholas Jarrot proved to be helpful. On December 9, Lewis returned to the Illinois side and met with Clark at Cahokia. He told Clark that Jarrot had a claim to a 400-acre tract at the mouth of Wood River called Rivière du Bois by the French settlers in the area,[6] which the latter had recommended as a good place to set up camp for the winter. While Clark went to take a look at the site (of which he approved), Lewis returned to St. Louis to resume his duties there. By now, a definite delineation of the duties of the two captains had evolved. Clark had become the day-to-day overseer of the party, while Lewis had assumed the political and diplomatic responsibilities for the expedition.

Clark and the party arrived at their potential camp on the Wood River about 2 o'clock in the afternoon of December 12. It was a windy day, and immediately after they landed it began to storm, with hail, snow, and a violent wind. In his journal, Clark wrote, "The hunders which I had sent out to examine the countrey in Deferent directions, returned with Turkies & oppossums and informed me the country was butifull and had great appearance of Gaim [game]."

Clark wasted no time. The next day, he selected a place to build huts, and set the men to clearing land and cutting logs. The fatiguing job of cabin-building became the prime occupation of the party until December 30. Then, the party's housing needs fulfilled, Clark finally moved into his own hut.

Beginning with the first day of their arrival at Camp Dubois, the men spent much of their time hunting. While many of the men were busy with cabin building and other jobs, others hunted. The journal entries indicate that between the day of the corps's arrival December 12, 1803, and May 14, 1804, at 4 p.m., when the party departed (a period of five months, or about 150 days), there are approximately twenty-seven entries which reported one or more of the men as having been out hunting, and, usually, with success. On two days, the men caught fish. The men probably went out hunting more often than the entries indicate during this period at Camp Dubois. Lewis was on his own at St. Louis most of the time, and Clark also was absent from camp during some periods, leaving Sergeant John Ordway in charge. This situation may explain, in part, why the records made that winter at times seem to be incomplete. In addition, Gary E. Moulton has suggested that the captains may not have considered it necessary to make daily entries during this period, since "they were not traveling and the expedition had not actually begun...."[7]

Although all of the men were good hunters, including Lewis and Clark, there are several who stand out as being exceptional. Drouillard was multi-talented, from the standpoint of qualities needed for the expedition. Not only was he an excellent frontiersman, scout, and interpreter, he was so highly esteemed as a hunter that he often is referred to in the journals simply as "the hunter." (On January 30, 1804, he shot 5 deer in one day.) Other outstanding hunters were Privates Reubin Field, Francois Labiche (whom Clark referred to as "the Indian"), Pierre Cruzatte, George Shannon, John Shields, Richard Windsor, William Werner, and Hugh McNeal. All of the guns used were flintlocks since percussion caps did not come into use until later. Many of the men had brought along their own personal guns, which they used in addition to those issued to them. The latter had been obtained mainly from the Harpers Ferry arsenal.

During their time at Camp Dubois, the men bagged grouse (perhaps the ruffed grouse), opossums, raccoons, many deer and turkeys, prairie fowl, catfish, squirrels, many rabbits, a wildcat, a loon (more likely a doublecrested cormorant), a muskrat, and a badger. It is not certain whether all of these "kills" were actually consumed. Undoubtedly, the meat obtained by the men through hunting (and, to a lesser extent, fishing) served as an important and tasty addition to their diet while at Camp Dubois. Hunting also provided the men with a meaningful outlet for their energy and certainly helped to alleviate their boredom.

By today's nutritional standards, these men would have needed only about half a pound (eight ounces) of meat a day, plus the vegetable protein obtained from bread/cereal products, to satisfy protein needs, assuming that their diet included enough food in addition to meat to satisfy total calorie needs. As discussed in Chapter 2, the standard army rations established in 1802 included 1¼ pounds of beef daily—which would provide over twice that amount. Had the men been forced to rely exclusively on hunting at Camp Dubois to obtain that amount of meat for each man daily (about fifty pounds for the group), the party would have needed to bag about 1.2 deer (or its equivalent in other game) daily.[8] During this time, any calorie needs exceeding those obtained from hunted game were supplied by provisions from nearby military sources. However, once they left Camp Dubois, the party had to focus on hunting, fishing, and foraging to supply both calorie and protein needs and to conserve their dried foods for emergencies later on. Going westward after leaving Fort Mandan with a party of thirty-two adults, as game became increasingly available, they began eating more and more meat, relying on it increasingly for both their caloric and protein needs. In his journal entry of July 13, 1805, Lewis estimated that the party required four deer, an Elk and a deer, or one buffalo, to supply the party plentifully for twenty-four hours. Paul S. Martin and Christine R. Szuter have calculated that, on the upper Missouri, between April 25 and July 13, 1805, the group actually was eating the equivalent of two buffaloes per day (about nine pounds per person).[9]

Only a few days after the party arrived at their prospective camp on Wood River, visitors began to come. Collectively, these visitors comprised a motley group—country people, farmers, traders, merchants, Indians, former army acquaintances of the captains, and others (both "mail and feemail," as Clark wrote in his inimitable spelling).[10] They usually brought small gifts (e.g., home-grown food or whiskey), and the captains reciprocated in kind by offering food or libations usually obtained from the commissary and/or by hunting. What little effect this generosity may have had on the party's food supply was far outweighed by the valuable information often obtained from the visitors. In fact, the exchange of information was advantageous to both the hosts and visitors.

These visitors are faceless folk, for Lewis and Clark did not have an artist accompanying them as did Prince Maximilian of Wied on his voyage up the Missouri in 1833. But by exercising a bit of imagination, one can visualize them quite well. The army acquaintances were people whom Lewis and/or Clark had known during their previous period of service in the United States Army. After retirement, these men had settled in the area for several reasons. At that time, military men were awarded land grants upon retirement. And plots along the Mississippi were attractive, especially those not far from St. Louis.

A large number of visitors were neighbor people who came to the camp for a variety of reasons, including curiosity and a need for socialization. In addition, there often was some other, sometimes hidden, agenda. But they came, and their visits provided the party with much-needed relief from the monotony and feelings of isolation which the men must have experienced.[11]

There are many journal entries which describe visits from neighborhood men who came to participate in shooting matches with members of the party. Sometimes they also brought things to sell. On January 1, Clark purchased six pounds of sugar for one dollar from one of the men who came to shoot.

Then there was Mrs. Cane, who came to visit on New Year's Day. Clark noted, "...a woman Came forward today wish to wash and doe Such things as may be necessary for the Detachment." On January 6, "...I ordered those men who had fought get Drunk & neglected Duty to go and build a hut for a Wo[man] who promises to wash & Sow &c." On February 5, Mrs. Cane called again, presumably because she knew that Captain Clark was sick. Finally, on April 15, Clark wrote, "Settled with Mrs. Cane for all to this day & paid 12/c [$12]."

Business people of the area were eager to cultivate the corps as potential buyers. They were aware that the group would have diverse needs and that the captains had authorization to charge all necessary purchases to the army. There were people from the commissary or the contractor (e.g., January 28, 1804) who came to discuss orders or to deliver same at intervals. Then, there were merchants from the area either soliciting business or delivering their wares, as well as people passing by in boats who also were desirous of selling their goods. In addition, local farmers were interested in selling their produce also (e.g., turnips, butter, and cheese).

On December 16, a pirogue arrived bearing a Mr. Samuel Griffith, whom Clark described as a "good farmer who lives nine miles up the Missouris." A Mr. Gilbert, a trader in salt, also came by. These men were the first of numerous visitors to come to Camp Dubois that winter. Mr. Griffith knew how to do business. Having paid Lewis and Clark a courtesy call on December 16, on the 23rd, according to Clark, he "Came down from his farm with a Load of Turnips &c. as a present to me...." Then, the next day Clark recorded, "I purchase a Cargo of Turnips for $3 a bushel from Mr. Gririffeth...."

In addition to food, the party gained other things from these visits. First, they did not want to live in isolation all winter at Camp Dubois. It was lonely there, and it was a laborious day's trip by canoe to St. Louis. Besides, they had duties to perform at camp, and Captain Clark allowed the men comparatively little freedom. Visitors broke the monotony. And, as newcomers to this western outpost, the men were eager to gain more information regarding the area and what it would be like going up the Missouri. In addition, the visitors brought news of political significance. St. Louis by this time was a hotbed of activity and intrigue, and it behooved the captains to keep posted on current developments. Finally, these interactions often led to the obtaining of provisions beyond those which were provided by the Commissary in St. Louis. All in all, it was advantageous to build a rapport with the surrounding inhabitants.

The journals contain numerous entries that describe Clark's obtaining food from neighbors during this period by giving them small items, or small amounts of money, in return. On December 23, Clark wrote, "I sent to Mr. Morrisons farm for a Teem & Corn, which arrived about 3 oClock." On January 4, he noted that he obtained tallow from Captain Whitesides who sold the beef to the commissary at $3 per hundred weight. On January 8, "a French man and his family come to see me today...I trade with them for Onions, and give him Tin &c...." On January 28, "Mr. Bagley came with potatos, fowl &c—I trade him. Mr. Cummins [Cummings] came with meel & Brandy from Contractor." On February 5, Clark reported that "Hanley Sent us Some Butter & milk...."[12]

Occasionally, Clark would send out one of the men to obtain specific items of food from some local farmer. On December 24, he sent Shields for some butter; the following day, the latter returned with four pounds of this staple, as well as "a cheese." On January 29, Clark wrote, "Express returned from Koho [Cahokia]: brought [some mail]. 8 bottles of wine Some Durant & files." On March 25, evidently in response to a request from Captain Clark, "Guterge [Goodrich] returned with Eggs...."[13] The procurement of food for the party obviously was a top priority of Clark's, and he seems to have been quite adept at finding out where various foods could be obtained. Further, the men themselves found creative ways to obtain additional food from the environment. That same day, Clark noted, "...the men find numers of Bee Trees & take great quantities of honey...."

It was important for the party to have a supply of salt, both as a seasoning and as a food preservative. In an undated note (probably between December 31 and January 3, 1803-04), Clark wrote that "a Salt works is established on a small River 30 miles up the river 10 miles from the Mississippi...." But there is no record of the party's actually procuring salt from this source. However, on May 4, 1804, when preparing for departure, Clark noted that he sent two men to St. Louis, partly for the purpose of obtaining salt. Clark's entry on May 9 stated, "Sent men up the Missouri for drinking water, it being much cooler than the Mississippi water." The corps was almost ready to leave Camp Dubois by then; they may have taken some of this water along.

From the day of their arrival at Wood River on December 12 until May 5, close to the day of their departure, the party had frequent visits from Indians. Some of them were local inhabitants who undoubtedly came, in part, out of curiosity or to avail themselves of the corps's hospitality. Others, for various reasons, had decided to camp in the vicinity for a while. Still others were simply passing through (usually going to or from St. Louis). Not long after he had landed on December 12, Clark had noticed that two canoes of Potawatomi Indians had come up on the other side and landed. Three of them came across in a small canoe, despite high waves and a violent wind. Clark commented that "...they were all drunk...."

On December 13 and 14, Clark wrote that some Indians had passed. On December 15, one Indian came with meat. The party soon learned that the Indians often gave the men some item of food as an opening overture, with the expectation that the recipient would respond fairly quickly in kind, offering a gift, also. Beneath these exchanges was the underlying desire on the part of both parties to obtain information of potential political significance. For example, on Christmas Day, 1803, three local Indians came to have dinner with the party. Clark gave them a bottle of whiskey, and they left after informing him that "all the nations were going to war against the Ozous [Osage?] in 3 months." This was valuable information for Clark, and well worth the dinner and whiskey.

On March 25, Clark wrote, "...at ll oClock 24 Sauckees [Sauk or Fox Indians] Come pass from St. Louis, and asked for Provisions.... I ordered them 75 lb. Beef, 25 lb. flour, & 50 lb. meal—." On March 26, he reported that he had visited the Indian camps. In one of them, he spied Simon Girty, an Indian sympathizer whom he had known since boyhood.[14] Clark continued, "Girtey has the Rhumertism verry bad...those Indians visit me in their turn, & as usial ask for Something. I give them flour &c." On March 27, Clark related, "Some Delways pass down to St. Louis (Simon Girty)...." Apparently, Girty was on a secret reconnaissance trip for the British.

On April 21, Clark wrote, "Mr. Chouteau arrived with 22 Indians, we Saluted them, and after Staying one [h]our, Cap. Lewis & myself Set out with them to St. Louis where we arrived before night." Clark returned to Camp on the night of April 25. On April 29, Clark reported, "Some Kickapoo Chiefs come down," apparently also going to St. Louis. On May 5, Clark reported, "a Sauckee Chief with 8 or 10 arrive & Stay all night 2 Perogus of Kickapoos return from St. Louis. I gave 4½ gals whisky & some Tobacco." This was obviously a diplomatic gesture, considering that the corps would soon be going up into Indian country.

Since it was customary during this period for army personnel to receive a daily ration of alcohol, it is not surprising that, on the evening of August 30, 1803, as Lewis was about to begin his trip down the Ohio, he wrote, "...gave my men some whiskey and retired to rest at 8 oClock...." Additional whiskey was sometimes given out under special circumstances. For example, a Detachment Order of February 20, 1804, issued by Lewis stated that, at Camp Dubois, during the absence of himself and Captain Clark from camp, the sawyers and the blacksmiths were to receive each an extra gill of whiskey per day, and be exempt from guard duty while engaged in these special pursuits. Moreover, the four men engaged in making sugar were to continue in that employment until further orders, and each was to receive a half a gill of extra whiskey per day and be exempt from guard duty. In these same orders, Lewis also ruled that "No whiskey shall in future be delivered from the Contractor's store except for the legal ration...."[15]

On special occasions, extra whiskey often was given out to the entire party. For example, when Captain Clark returned from a visit to St. Louis on April 13, he rewarded the men with "Lead, Powder, & an extra gill of Whiskey —." In fact, this practice continued after leaving Camp Dubois up until July 4, 1805, at the mouth of the Yellowstone River when the corps had the bittersweet experience of celebrating this holiday with the last of the party's stock of whiskey (see Chapters 5 and 6).

The party's consumption of alcohol (mainly whiskey), seems to have been confined chiefly to the liquor given them daily by the sergeant of their mess, their "legal ration." Drinking four shots of whiskey daily may seem a bit generous by today's standards. But heavy drinking had been customary in America from Colonial times up though the post-Revolutionary period and continuing into the nineteenth century, and the army's liquor allowances reflect this custom.[16]

During the winter at Camp Dubois, there were several recorded incidents involving illegal consumption of liquor by some of the men. As early as November 18, Lewis and Clark, coming back to the boat after an excursion, "found a number of our men who had left camp contrary to instructions & drunk, had much difficulty in geten [into the boat?]." On December 31, 1803, Clark wrote: "I issued certain [orders?] & prohibited a Certain Ramey from Selling Liquor to the Party...." And, on March 3, 1804, in Detachment Orders, Lewis stated that "...to such as have made hunting or other business a pretext to cover their design of visiting a neighboring whiskey shop," he could not grant permission to go into the country.[17]

Around the holidays, things seemed to get worse. On December 31, 1803, Clark noted that "Colter, Willard Leakens Hall & Collins Drunk." On January 6, he ordered these men to "go and build a hut for a woman...." (presumably Mrs. Cane, discussed earlier.) Then on January 15, he wrote, "Seven or eight men were intoxicated from the whiskey they had received from Major Rumsey out of the whiskey barrel, while following the [commissary's] waggon on its way out to Camp." On January 16, Clark charged Rumsey for the 30 gills of whiskey due the party, "which he payd." On April 16, several men were confined for drunkenness.[18] Drunkenness would have been expected among a group of thirty enlisted men ranging in age from seventeen (George Shannon) to thirty-five (John Shields), particularly since heavy drinking was common in America during this period. Things might have been worse had the men not enjoyed such activities as hunting and engaging in shooting matches while at Camp Dubois.

Already in early February the captains were turning their attention to the trip up the Missouri. On February 7, Clark noted, "The Creek or River à Dubois raisin fast...if the present fresh continues a few days, the water passing down the Small river [the Dubois] will Wash off all that immence quantity of mud which has filled up its mouth for 300 yards by the Missouries ooze or mud...." Departure would have been delayed while this mud remained. On March 22, Clark wrote, "Set the workmen to work on the Boat."

Between March 26 and April 17, 1804 there are several entries which deal with the parching of corn and converting it to meal in preparation for the trip up the Missouri. On March 26, Clark reported that it is "a verry Smokey day I had Corn parched to make parched meal, workmen all at work prepareing the Boat...." Next day, on the 27th, he had "all hands parching Corn &c...beating at two mortars parched corn."

By this time, the party was preparing in earnest to depart Camp Dubois. The smoke to which Clark referred was probably coming from the fires which the men had made in order to heat the corn to the high temperature required for parching. This process served two purposes. First, scorching the grain prevented its sprouting; thus it could be stored safely. Second, parching the grain resulted in the hulls becoming separated from the kernel. After the hulls were removed (by flailing and winnowing), the kernels then could be pounded or ground into a meal or flour. Hulled corn (Table 5.1) had excellent keeping qualities and could be used en route for making various corn dishes, including hominy, grits, and cornmeal mush.

In England, during the Celtic Iron Age, various mechanical devices (also called mortars) were developed for use on a small scale for pounding or grinding grains. Clark's statement "beating at two mortars parched corn" would seem to imply that the men were grinding this batch of corn into meal, using just such a hand-powered mechanical device, after first removing the hulls by "beaten with flails and winnowing with fans."[19] In any case, they were using out-moded equipment, for grist mills had been used in America since early Colonial times.[20] And since there were grist mills on the Missouri at this time,[21] undoubtedly there were some in the Camp Dubois area as well.

The question arises, why were the men not using a grist mill for this task? First, it probably had not been feasible to erect a mill at Camp Dubois for their short stay. Second, considering that this was a small batch of unparched corn, it may not have been feasible to haul it elsewhere for grinding either. Meanwhile, there were quite a few men around the camp, often with little to do. Clark probably decided that they would be better off grinding corn, albeit by an inefficient, outdated method, than to be idle. On April 2, Clark reported, "...all mess arranged, & men makeing Parched meal...." Then, on April 23, he wrote "I have meal mad & the flour Packed & repacked." On April 17, he wrote his last word on the subject: "...also packed...one bu Parched [corn] of inferior quality."

It is a great enigma that, while the party was at Camp Dubois, Captain Clark apparently was doing an admirable job directing the party and getting ready for the expedition, despite being plagued by health problems. Over a twenty-eight-day period, January 10 through February 6, Clark made fourteen separate entries in which he described himself as sick, unwell, or that "My head aches much." However, except for January 10, when he reported that he had almost frozen his feet when he broke through the ice of a pond while exploring an Indian fortification (Cahokia Mounds) the previous day, Clark never describes his illnesses. While at Camp Dubois, Clark made several references to visits made by a Dr. Hanson Catlett (Catlate), who was a surgeon's mate for Amos Stoddard's company in St. Louis in 1804. Clark never stated what his mission was, but Dr. Catlett probably was making routine visits to Camp Dubois to check on the men's health.

On April 1, 1804, Clark reported that "Dr. Catlate's Boat arrived with provisions." He then noted that Lewis had gone back to St. Louis with Dr. Catlett on business. Earlier, on March 30, Clark had written that "Priors [Pryor] is verry Sick". But, considering the slowness of communications between the Camp and St. Louis, it is doubtful that Dr. Catlett knew about Pryor's illness before his arrival April 1. On April 2, Clark reported three men sick, one of whom could have been Pryor, but he does not describe their condition. On April 3, he wrote, "...Capt Lewis return with Dr. Catlate...." Again, it hardly seems possible that Dr. Catlett had been apprised that these three men were ill. On April 6, Clark reported "Sgt. Pryor Still Sick...."

On May 8, Clark notes "Dr. Catlate's" presence at the Camp again; on the next day, he states that "..Dr. Catlet Set out late for St. Louis." On May 11 or 12, Dr. Catlet must have returned to the camp because Clark's entry for May 12 reads, "Doct. Catlett set out at ll oClock." It seems likely that some of these visits were for the purpose of checking on Captain Clark, who seemed to be chronically unwell, or to examine the three men who were sick. As a surgeon's mate, it is highly likely that his May 8 visit could have involved an over-all checkup on the men's physical condition prior to their departure, which Dr. Catlett, by that date, would have realized was imminent. Clark's failure to describe the illnesses of himself and those of his men, and to explain the reasons for Dr. Catlett's visits, could have stemmed from a desire to de-emphasize the illnesses of the party.

By March 25, the corps was making final preparations for departure. That day, Clark wrote in his journal, "The musquetors are verry bad this evening"—a sure sign of spring. On March 31, he noted that "...Majr Runsy [Nathan Rumsey] arrived." Then, on May 3, he referred to Rumsey again: "Major Rumsey was polite enough to examine all my provisions. Several Kegs of Pork he Condemed."

By April 1, 1804, spring had definitely arrived at Camp Dubois, and the men were bursting with the desire to depart. But the party still had much to accomplish before the men could begin their voyage. Lewis realized that, since his party was larger than he first had anticipated, he needed more provisions as well as time to procure them. And there were many other tasks he, Captain Clark, and the men needed to complete.

On April 3, Clark wrote, "I have the flour packed and repacked. also some porkie, packed in barrels..."(probably in salt or salt brine). On April 4, he made this entry: "all day packing Provision Setled account with the Contractor for all the Issuses to the first of the month & what Provisions he had furnished."

On April 14 and 16, Clark reported packing the food items listed in Table 5.1, which had been purchased the previous weekend in St. Louis. During the remainder of the month, Clark continued to pack and re-pack the boat.[22] Finally, he called on Mr. Hay, the postmaster at nearby Cahokia, to assist him in packing, over the last three days of April. Mr. Hay apparently was considered to be somewhat of an expert with respect to this endeavor. On May 8, Clark loaded the keelboat and one perogue, and the following day, he and twenty oarsmen took it for a ride on the Mississippi to check its balance. On May 11, seven "french men" arrived, followed by an eighth, on May 13. These men probably were the *engagés* who were hired to man the boats going up the Missouri.

On Sunday, May 13, Clark wrote that he "despatched an express this morning to Capt. Lewis at St. Louis...all our provisions goods and equipage on Board of a Boat of 22 oars, a [party], a large Perogue of 7 oares [in which eight French] a Second Perogue of 6 oars, [Soldiers] Complete with Sails &c. &c. [the large pirogue was red, the second pirogue, white.] The latter perogue carried Corporal Warfington and his squad of five soldiers, who were expected to return from somewhere up the Missouri before winter.[23] The men had been at Camp Dubois on the Wood River for five months. On the next day, May 14, 1804, the corps would begin its journey.

Chapter 5
From St. Louis to the Pacific and Back

On May 14, at 4 o'clock in the afternoon, the Corps of Discovery set out from Camp Dubois on the Wood River near St. Louis. The party of about fifty men, who had been chosen with care, departed in a flat-bottomed keelboat and two pirogues, sailed across the Mississippi, and ascended the Missouri a few miles before stopping for the night. Like most explorers and pioneers, they were far from certain where they were going, how long they would be gone, or what perils they might encounter en route. And certainly they were not sure just how they were going to subsist during this journey (Figure 5.1).

Captains Lewis and Clark were acutely aware that, despite the importance of their weapons, ammunition, and other supplies, without an adequate food supply, the expedition would collapse. So they had made what preparations they could, knowing that for the most part they would have to live off the land. There was no way that they could pack enough for the trip even if they could have predicted its duration. First, there were the limitations of space. The main boat was a keelboat, strongly resembling a Spanish river galley, only fifty-five feet long and eight feet wide. It could accommodate only ten tons of supplies, including food. Then there was the ongoing problem of spoilage. This problem forced the men to delay the final assembling of food provisions until shortly before their departure from Wood River. It clearly was impossible to take along fresh fruits, vegetables, and fresh meats. Essentially, their staples had to be those which were salted or dried. When they departed, they were carrying about eight tons of such items, including flour, ground meal, salt pork, and 193 pounds of concentrated portable soup. These staples were to be used mainly as a supplement to the game and other foods obtained by the men during the expedition. They had neither the space nor sterilizing techniques for bringing along a supply of potable water, which forced them to rely on water from the river en route.

Table 5.1 shows a memorandum prepared by Clark shortly before the group departed on their journey, which lists these provisions. Another notation in the journals shows that one-hundred gallons of whiskey also were procured for the men, plus an additional twenty gallons of whiskey that was intended to serve as gifts for Indians they expected to encounter.

Unquestionably, the daily staples made eating monotonous. In order to make the meals more interesting, they were offered alternate menus: one day, "lyed corn and grece was issued; the next day, poark and flour; and the day following, indian meal and poark." No pork was issued when there was fresh meat on hand. So the real element of surprise was provided by the hunters. Each evening, after their boats were "brought to," and the ration of staples distributed, Sergeant Ordway would divide up any fresh meat that the hunters had obtained that day (plus any fresh fruits or berries collected from the countryside). Thus no two day's rations were ever alike. Each man also was rewarded at this time with a gill (four ounces) of whiskey, which was part of the army ration during this period.

No cooking was allowed during the day. "Cooking on the march" would have been too time-consuming, delaying the party's progress. And, considering the unsteadiness of the

Figure 5.1 From Camp Dubois to Fort Mandan, 1804. From Fort Mandan to St. Louis, 1806. *Cartography by Dr. Steven Dutch.*

boat, having pots and pans rolling around on the deck would have been disruptive and potentially dangerous. But no cooking during the day also meant that both breakfast and lunch consisted of cold leftovers from the previous evening's meal.

In the morning, while most of the men were breaking camp and loading the boats, George Drouillard, the lead hunter, and usually two to five others of the party would set out by land in search of game and edible plant foods. They led two horses along the banks of the river for the purpose of bringing home game.

The journals provide much useful information regarding the foods on which the men subsisted as they ascended the Missouri. During June and July, as spring was evolving into summer, seasonal foods became available. This was berry time on the Missouri, and the fruits available during this time included grapes, the Osage plum, gooseberries, raspberries, wild apples, vast quantities of mulberries, along with crab apples and the wild cherry of the Missouri. On June 5, Clark wrote that his black servant, York, obtained greens for the party by swimming from the boat to a sand bar, then swimming back with a quantity of wild cresses or Tung (tongue) grass. On June 12, the party had bought 300 pounds of buffalo "grease," or tallow, from traders on two rafts. Undoubtedly, it was purchased for the purpose of making pemmican, used by Indians and traders and valued for its excellent keeping qualities. Although not specifically mentioned in the journals during this time period, some of the berries which became available during the summer undoubtedly were also used in the making of pemmican.

In the Missouri area, they obtained deer, elk, and bear, plus one wolf. In mid-July, entering the Nebraska area near the Platte River, the hunters obtained mainly deer. By July 22, in the Omaha/Council Bluffs area, they caught their first catfish. The party remained there during late July and early August, trying to arrange a council with neighboring tribes to tell them the news of the Louisiana Purchase and the desire of the United States for friendship.

For the rest of the summer, the party found fruit and catfish to be plentiful, along with reasonable amounts of game. The fruits included grapes, plums, and a delicious currant-like fruit called rabbit-berry, in the Indians' language. While going up the Missouri, the party's consumption of calories, protein, and the vitamins and minerals associated with meat probably was adequate. Berries and other fruit would have provided them with needed vitamin C. However, there were other nutritional lacks, as discussed below in Chapter 6.

The stay in the Council Bluffs area marked the beginning of much ceremonial activity between Indians and the party. It served several valuable purposes, including the obtaining of needed food. In exchange, the men presented the Indians with various small presents.

On August 16, still awaiting the council, the men made use of their time by sweeping Maha Creek using a drag made with small willows and bark. An astounding total of 1,118 fish was obtained using this technique. This catch included an exotic variety of fish, many whose origins were thought to be the Ohio River or the lower Mississippi. It would have been wise for the party to have dried or salted what could not be consumed immediately from this huge fish catch. But their doing so is not noted specifically in the journals. Sometimes, but not always, the men made "jerky" of any excess meat. Occasionally, they made jerky when it was too windy to travel and time was available.

On August 20, Sergeant Charles Floyd died near Sioux City, Iowa, presumably of a burst appendix and subsequent peritonitis (see Chapter 6).

Table 5.1 A Memorandum of Articles in readiness for the Voyage* [Clark - undated, ca. May 14, 1804]			Lbs.
Viz:	14	Bags of Parchmeal	1200
	9	Bags of Common meal	800
	11	Bags Corn Hulled	1000
	30	half Barrels of flour; 3 Bags of flour	3400
	7	Bags of Biscuit; 4 Barrels Biscuit	560
	7	Barrels of Salt	750
	50	Kegs of Pork	3705
	2	Boxes of Candles, incl. 50 lb. soap	170
	1	Bag of Candle-wick	8
	1	Bag of Coffee	50
	1	Bag of Beens & 1 of Pees	100
	2	Bags of Sugar	112
	1	Keg of Hogs Lard	70
	4	Barrels of Corn hulled	600
	1	Barrel of meal	150
		Grees [Grease]	600
	50	bushels meal	
	24	Natchies Corn Huled [Hulled]	
	21	Bales of Indian goods	
		Tools of every Description, etc.	

*Adapted from Moulton, 1986(2): 217-18.

On August 23, beyond the mouth of the Big Sioux River, in what is now South Dakota, the men killed their first buffalo, on the prairie to the north.

On September 11, a man was observed riding on horseback towards the boat; the men were pleased to see that it was George Shannon, the youngest member of the group, who had been missing almost a month. He had been dispatched after their two horses who had strayed away August 16, and he later had become lost. During the first four days, he had exhausted his bullets, and then nearly starved to death, subsisting for twelve days on a few grapes and a rabbit which he killed by making use of a hard piece of stick for a ball. He had been at the point of killing his horse for food when he fortunately sighted and rejoined the party.

On September 15, pronghorn antelope ("goats") and great quantities of buffalo were seen near the confluence of the White River with the Missouri. These two types of animals proved to be very important sources of food for the men during the next weeks and months.

On the 17th of September, Captain Lewis reported seeing "immense herds of Buffaloe, deer Elk and Antelope which we saw in every direction feeding on the hills and plains. I do not think I exaggerate when I estimate the number of Buffaloe...at one view to amount to 3000." By September 18, continuing northward, the men also were seeing deer. That day, Lewis wrote, "the hunters Killed 10 Deer to day and a Prarie wolf, had it all jurked & Skins Stretch after Camping."

By September 26, they had encountered the Teton Indians, who invited them to a celebration including a dance in their council house. A large fire in which they were cooking provisions stood near, and in the center was about 400 pounds of excellent buffalo meat—a present for the group. The meal consisted of the dog which they had just been cooking, a great dish among the Sioux and used at all festivals. There also was pemmican—made of buffalo meat, dried or jerked, and then pounded and mixed raw with grease. In return, the two chiefs were given a peck of corn and a carrot of tobacco as presents.[1]

By early October, the party had arrived in Mandan country, in what is now North Dakota. The party noted much evidence of advanced horticulture now, and rabbit-berries became prevalent again. On October 12, the Mandan welcomed the men with much ceremony. Captain Clark wrote that at the village of the third Chief the latter presented the party with about "ten bushels of corn, Some beens & [s]quashes all of which we accepted with pleasure." Later, when the chiefs came on board the boat, the captains gave them "Some Sugar, a little Salt, and a SunGlass."[2] Later, the Indians also brought them presents of goat's flesh and buffalo meat.

By November 2, Lewis had found a good site for the fort three miles down river where the men began building their huts for the winter. By November 21, the party was settled in its new winter habitation, where they awaited the first return of spring in order to continue their journey. It was fortunate that the men had been able to move in by then; already there had been frosts and ice on the river for almost two weeks.

During the next four months, there was much bartering with the Indians, who wanted to exchange corn and occasionally beans and squashes for small articles, the repair of axes, kettles, and other utensils, and other favors. The latter included the treatment of the Indians for various health problems which they were experiencing during the corps's stay at Fort Mandan. There was intermittent killing of buffalo, followed by periods of scarcity for the party and Indians alike. At such times, the men had to confine themselves to a vegetable diet, supplemented at times with their salt pork. Ordinarily, the principal food for the Indians in winter was the buffalo, with their corn, beans, and other vegetable foods being reserved for summer, or as a last resource against a possible attack from the Sioux. Because of the fear of the Sioux the party and the Indians went hunting in groups; sometimes the Indians and corps members hunted together. But these tactics usually resulted in the buffalo being obtained in such large quantities that the meat tended to become wasted through failure to dry it and/or from using inadequate storage methods. In addition to their other responsibilities, the captains attended to the health needs of the Indians, as well as members of the party. Chapter 6 provides a detailed discussion of food and health issues involving both the Mandans and the corps while the party wintered at Fort Mandan.

By late February, 1805, the party was working to disengage the boats which had been frozen in the ice during the winter. The men also were preparing tools to build boats for their voyage, having realized that small canoes and dugouts would be much more convenient than the barge in continuing their journey up the Missouri, once the ice was out of the river.

As winter ended, despite intermittent periods of mild food scarcity and various health problems, the men had survived. Their interactions with the Mandans had been mutually advantageous. Soon they would resume their journey.

At 4 o'clock in the afternoon, on April 7, 1805, the Corps of Discovery began its journey toward the Pacific Ocean (Figure 5.2). Although the trip from St. Louis up the Missouri

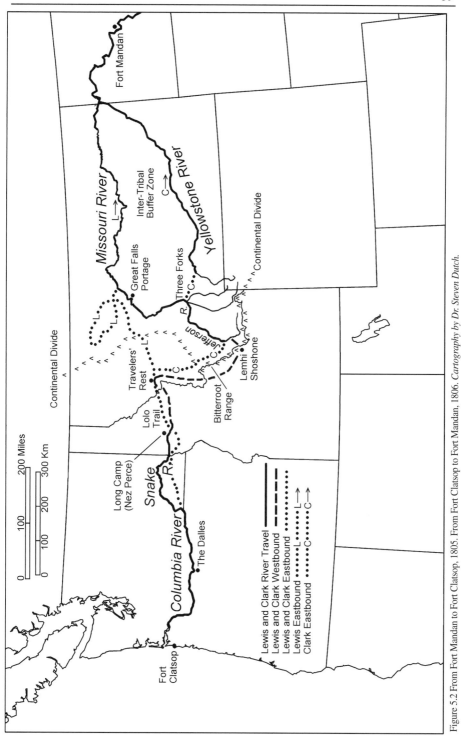

Figure 5.2 From Fort Mandan to Fort Clatsop, 1805. From Fort Clatsop to Fort Mandan, 1806. *Cartography by Dr. Steven Dutch.*

to Fort Mandan had marked a new experience for the party, they had not been following an uncharted path. Various traders had been going up and down that part of the Missouri and had shared their knowledge with others, including Captains Lewis and Clark. But now, the party was about to enter an area where little white exploration had occurred. The Mandans and Hidatsa on the Missouri had some knowledge of this area, and they had shared this information with Lewis and Clark during the winter months.

Going upstream from St. Louis to Mandan country, the men had coped with the chronic problem of sand bars and thick mud. Over the winter, the Indians had kept warning them that this problem would become progressively worse as they went west. So the captains decided to send the keelboat back to St. Louis with a small crew of nine men under the command of Corporal Warfington. Since they planned to proceed now with just two large dugouts and six small canoes, their space for carrying food would be much more limited. There are no lists or descriptions of the food taken along on this segment of the journey. But, judging from subsequent entries, the party took along still unused staples from their original supply, plus the remainder of their whiskey. And, as before, their non-perishable food would be used only as a supplement to the meat and other food they would have to obtain by daily hunting and foraging. Their party now included Toussaint Charbonneau, a French-Canadian interpreter whom they had met soon after their arrival in Mandan country. With him were his sixteen-year old Shoshone wife, Sacagawea, and their infant son, Jean Baptiste.

The corps had been in Mandan country six months. Their stay at Fort Mandan was unique, in part because the men remained there for a longer period than at any of their subsequent sojourns during the trip. They had become well acquainted with the area and had developed more meaningful relationships with the Mandans than with other Indians encountered later.

Leaving Fort Mandan was truly a great moment for the corps. All that had gone before had served merely as prelude to what they now were about to attempt. After the journey was underway, the first mention of food came on the third day, April 9, when Lewis suggested halting for dinner. At this time, Sacagawea busied herself looking for mouse nests. She was searching for the wild artichoke, which the mice collect and deposit in large hoards in their nests. She procured a good quantity of these roots for the men in this way. On April 11, George Drouillard went out hunting and came back with a deer. It was especially welcome, since the party had obtained no fresh meat for several days, presumably because of overhunting by the Hidatsa and Assiniboin Indians in the area.[3]

Very soon, they began to see more signs of the game that they had anticipated, and the party's hunters were ready for the challenge. Although Drouillard was acknowledged as the lead hunter, Lewis and Clark and numerous others in the party were also skilled hunters. By April 18, Clark reported that the game, such as buffalo, elk, antelope and deer were "very plenty."

On April 22, Lewis and Clark walked on shore to the White Earth River, now known as the Little Muddy, at Williston, North Dakota. Here, Lewis ascended to the top of a bluff and surveyed "immense herds of buffaloe, elk, deer, & antelopes feeding in one common and boundless pasture." They now began to see similar scenes almost daily, causing Lewis to remark confidently one day, "I believe that two good hunters could conveniently supply a regiment with provisions." By May 6, he was actually boasting, saying that

"...it is now only amusement for Captain Clark and myself to kill as much meat as the party can consume."

En route from the Yellowstone to the Musselshell, on April 29, the men bagged their first grizzly, a young male of about 300 pounds. It was the first of many grizzlies that they would kill during their trip. The men soon learned that this animal was extremely dangerous and difficult to kill. And they began to appreciate why the Indians feared it. In fact, they learned never to hunt this animal alone. Fortunately for the men, the grizzly never climbs trees. Its weight likely would cause most tree branches to break. This characteristic of grizzlies later enabled some of the men to escape safely from them by climbing a tree.

On May 8, Lewis wrote, "We *nooned it* just above the entrance of a large river...," indicating that the party stopped and had lunch. He related that the wild licorice was very abundant there, as well as the wild apple or breadroot. The latter, he said, "forms a considerable article of food for the Indians of the Missouri...." In Clark's version of this same event, he reports that Sacagawea gathered both the wild licorice root and the white apple, "and gave me to eat...."

Like the good administrators they were, the captains were quick to discern the strengths and weaknesses of each member of the corps, and they attempted to play to their strengths as much as possible. They soon observed that Toussaint Charbonneau did not do well in crisis situations, e.g., handling the pirogues under windy conditions. However, he was valuable to the corps as an interpreter and was an excellent cook. Upon leaving Fort Mandan, the crew began sleeping in tents at night, with the party divided into four groups. Each tent had its own mess and head cook. The captains shared their tent with the three Charbonneaus and Drouillard, with Toussaint serving as cook. Sergeants Gass, Ordway, and Pryor were in charge of the other three messes. On May 9, Toussaint Charbonneau was asked by Lewis to make *boudin blanc* ("white pudding"), a Cajun sausage, for the entire group. That day, en route from the Yellowstone to the Musselshell River, Captain Lewis had killed a buffalo cow, from which he saved the best of the meat as well as the intestines for Charbonneau. Engagingly referring to him as "our wrighthand cook," he immediately got Charbonneau started with the task of preparing this succulent delicacy. After kneading the cut-up meat with pepper, salt, and flour, Charbonneau stuffed the mixture into the intestines. Lewis wrote that it was then "baptized in the missouri with two dips and a flirt, and bobbed into the kettle." Next, it was boiled, then fried with bear's oil until brown. It was then eaten with delight by the party.[4]

Upon reaching the mouth of the Musselshell on May 20, they seemed to be moving into a new ecosystem with less grass and smaller game. In his journal Clark wrote that there now was "but little vegetation of any kind except the prickley pear,... little grass...[and] game not as abundant as below...." On May 25, Captain Clark killed his first ibex or bighorn. They were seeing more of the bighorn now, along with elk, and less of the buffalo. Paul S. Martin and Christine R. Szuter have noted that "From the mouth of the Yellowstone to Great Falls, the only part of the Missouri not supporting big game in large numbers was a strip above the mouth of the Musselshell River, where sterile soils known to fur traders as the *Mauvaises Terres* (the Badlands) yielded little forage."[5] Nevertheless, the party continued to obtain plenty of meat (mainly in the form of smaller game) until reaching Three Forks. This plenitude was evidenced by Captain Lewis's entry of July 13, where he wrote that "We eat an immensity of meat." In fact, he estimated that "it requires 4 deer, an Elk and a deer, or one buffaloe, to supply us plentifully twenty-four hours. Meat now forms our food principally as we reserve our flour, parched meal and corn as much as possible for the rocky mountains which we are shortly to enter, and where from the indian account [the Hidatsa near Fort Mandan], game is not very abundant."

On June 2, the party came to the mouth of a major fork of the Missouri on the starboard side. They named this fork the Marias River after a cousin of Captain Lewis. After much reconnoitering and debate, they decided to take the southwest fork. On June 13, Lewis, going on ahead with a few men, heard the sounds of falls and saw spray arising like a column of smoke. He knew it had to be the Great Falls which the Hidatsa had described, and he was greatly relieved. On June 14, the entire party arrived at the Great Falls, where the canoes and supplies would need to be portaged around the five cascades and intervening rapids. A survey of the area indicated that the portaging distance would be about eighteen miles, which the men optimistically estimated would take about half a day. Instead, it took about a month, causing considerable delay. While most of the men were involved in portaging, others were engaged in hunting and fishing to provide food for the party.

After leaving Mandan in April, the general health of the corps had been quite good for about two months, but, by early June, an avalanche of health concerns and complaints was developing. The men seemed to have lost weight, neither Lewis nor Clark was feeling well, and many of the men were suffering from constipation and/or other digestive complaints. Sacagawea was sick for ten days, beginning June 10, from what later was diagnosed as pelvic inflammatory disease. From late April to July 15, the men had been eating copious amounts of meat. One might wonder whether, during this period when food (and calories) had been most plentiful, the party should have been at its healthiest. In fact, as just noted, the party's health had worsened. (See Table 6.1 for a dietary assessment of this period.)

There had been a brief pause for celebration on July 4. Lewis wrote, "...we gave the men a drink of sperits, it being the last of our stock...."[6] Then, on July 15, having made a successful portage, the men proceeded in search of the source of the Missouri. They also were looking for the Shoshones, who thus far had evaded them. They desperately needed to make contact with them in order to obtain horses for the trek over the mountains ahead. The party now proceeded with eight canoes, having constructed two more canoes while at the portage site to carry their belongings and supplies.

On July 25, Clark noted that he and a party of four men had proceeded on a few miles to the Three Forks of the Missouri. The next day, Clark and two of the men proceeded to the top of a mountain which afforded a good view of the Three Forks. They were joined by Lewis and the rest of the party two days later. The captains decided to name the forks the Jefferson, the Madison, and the Gallatin, after the current president, secretary of state, and secretary of the treasury. They had made it to the Divide: an important goal had been realized. Now, the corps needed to cross the Divide in order to reach a navigable tributary of the Columbia River.

Having reached the Three Forks, Lewis and Clark decided that the party now would proceed up the Jefferson and that Lewis would go on ahead with a few men, continuing to look for the Shoshones. On August 12, while on this exploratory mission, Lewis decided to ascend to the top of a dividing ridge, from which he could see immense ranges of high mountains further west. Then, descending the far side of this mountain about ¾ of a mile, he found a running creek with cold, clear water. Here he paused, and took a drink. Lewis had just gone over what is now known as Lemhi Pass; he had crossed the Continental Divide.

Lewis reveled in that first drink of what he called "the Great Columbia River," actually a tiny headwater stream of the Lemhi River, which is part of the Columbia watershed. But the moment undoubtedly was marred by the view he had just obtained from the ridge. Looking west, Lewis had seen further ranges of mountains, which told him that portage to the Columbia River proper was going to be difficult. Now he was more convinced than ever that finding the Shoshones and obtaining horses was crucial if the party was going to get over those mountains. He needed to get back to Clark and the rest of the party as soon as possible so that they could proceed over the Divide together. But right now he and his men had an even more immediate problem. That morning Lewis and his three men had breakfasted on the last of their venison, with only a small piece of pork left in reserve. It turned out that they had failed to get any game on the way back, so upon their return over the Divide the evening of August 15 the only food they had left was a pound of flour, which they stirred into boiling water to make a gruel.

The good part about the trip back was that on August 13 they finally met some Shoshones, three females. The women were very frightened, but Lewis's friendly behaviors, including gifts of trinkets, seemed to allay their anxiety. Then, with the help of Drouillard and his sign language Lewis was able to communicate with them. Ultimately, they led him to their people who were camped on the Lemhi River. Their chief was Cameahwait, who turned out to be Sacagawea's brother. Although he was friendly, his people were suspicious that the expedition party might be friends of their enemies, the Blackfeet Indians, and Lewis was afraid that the Shoshones might flee in alarm into the mountains, leaving the corps stranded there for the winter. But, by using a variety of enticements, he got them to cross the Lemhi Pass and wait at the Forks of the Beaverhead (Jefferson) until Clark's party arrived on August 17.

The actual crossing of the Divide took only one day (August 26), but the preparations preceding it, coupled with the party's stay at the Shoshone camp on the Lemhi River afterward, consumed a period of twenty-three days (August 9-31, 1805). During this period, the captains were busy executing critical political maneuvers with Chief Cameahwait in order to obtain the necessary horses and, hopefully, a knowledgeable Shoshone guide to help them in getting over the forbidding Bitterroot Mountains.

Throughout this period, the men had gone out hunting every day, but there was little food to be had in this area, except grouse and some roots and berries. And the party's food staples had become very low. On August 19, in a desperate attempt to augment their scanty food supply, Lewis had a seine, a net constructed of willow bark, set out to catch some trout. Happily, the seine yielded 528 fish, most of which Lewis distributed to the Indians. This gave all of the group, large though it was, at least one good meal before going back over the Divide.

According to Chief Cameahwait, the rugged Bitterroot Mountains were hardly accessible to either man or beast. But he added an encouraging piece of information. There was an elderly Indian at his camp, he said (whom the men later named "Old Toby"), who knew of a route over the ranges, one that the Nez Perces used each year when they crossed over it to hunt the buffalo down on the plains. Ultimately, Old Toby agreed to guide the party in crossing them.

The party left the Shoshone camp on September 1 to go over the Bitterroots. But to get to them, Old Toby first had to take them on a circuitous route, whereby they ultimately crossed the Bitterroots via the rugged Lolo Trail. Winter comes early in these mountains.

As the elevation increased, it was getting colder, and some days, it snowed. On September 3, Clark noted that there was little to eat but grouse. The food supply had become so low that the party consumed the last of its salt pork that day. Fortunately, next day, at the Bitterroot River, the captains met a band of friendly Salish Indians who shared with them their limited food supply of berries and roots. These roots were undoubtedly bitterroots. It is ironic that this plant, whose beautiful blooms have become Montana's state flower, should have such a bitter taste. The men did not like the bitterroots, and there is no mention that they ever searched for them during the trip over the Bitterroots. Instead, they focused on securing game but with little success.

On September 6, going north along the Bitterroot River, they had nothing to eat but two grouse and some berries for thirty-three people. On September 11, they finally got started up Lolo Pass, over the Bitterroots. Over the four-day period of September 14-17, the food situation became so serious that the men were forced to kill their three colts, one at a time, for food. They reasoned that if they had to sacrifice some of their horses the colts were the most expendable.

There were no more colts now. Both the horses and the party were starving and physically exhausted. The captains were facing a serious dilemma. They finally decided that Clark should set out with six hunters and go on ahead to level country to hunt and then send food back to the party. So, on September 18, the advance party started out; Lewis and the others were to follow behind. That night, Lewis finally broke out "a Skant proportion" of the portable soup, of which they had only a few canisters left.

On September 19, Lewis got his party going shortly after sunrise. After six miles, "the ridge terminated [at today's Sherman Peak] and to [their] inexpressible joy [they] discovered a large tract of Prairie Country lying to the S.W...." They had sighted the end of the Bitterroots! But the prairie they had just seen was still about sixty miles away. They had to keep going. On September 22, Lewis embarked on what he called a forced march to the open country. At about two and a half miles, the party met Reubin Field bringing them dried fish and camas roots that Clark had obtained from some Nez Perce Indians at Weippe Prairie. They consumed this food with relish, then proceeded to a village of friendly Nez Perce Indians, reaching it at 5 p.m. It had taken them about eleven days to get over the Bitterroots proper, although the entire enterprise had consumed the latter part of August and much of September.

Moulton and other historians believe that the trip over the Bitterroot Mountains via the Lolo Trail was the most severe test of the expedition.[7] It is indeed a tribute to the outstanding leadership of Lewis and Clark that the party was able to triumph over the Rocky Mountains and that the captains had managed to keep morale from collapsing.

It turned out that both Clark and his party, as well as Lewis and his men, became sick from the dried fish and roots which they had received from the Nez Perce. Most of the men became violently ill for a week or more with acute diarrhea and vomiting. There has been much speculation as to the exact cause of this illness. I offer my own assessment of the diet and health of the men after the Bitterroot experience in Chapters 6 and 7.

Twisted Hair, one of the Nez Perce chiefs with whom the captains developed a strong friendship, proved to be very helpful to them. Drawing a map on a white elk skin, he showed them how the creek they were on emptied into the Clearwater, which was then joined from the northeast by the North Fork of the Clearwater. The latter then flowed west to join the Snake, which then poured into the Columbia. But before they could resume their trek westward, they had to find trees big enough to make canoes.

For a week Lewis was bedridden, recovering from the above mentioned illness, and during that time Clark moved camp to the junction of the North Fork of the Clearwater with the main stream. Here, they began to make dugouts from large pines, probably the Ponderosa, "burning out the holler of [their] Canoes." It took ten days to complete four large canoes and one small one. By October 6, the canoes were finished. The next day, Clark had the canoes put in the water and loaded. At last they were ready to tackle the final leg of their journey to the Pacific.

On October 7, the party started down the Clearwater River toward the west. The expedition was once again waterborne, going downstream for the first time since Lewis had turned the keelboat from the Ohio into the Mississippi River two years earlier in the fall of 1803. On October 10, they reached the place where the Clearwater flows into the Snake River at what is now Lewiston, Idaho, on the Idaho border. Here, the men bought fish from the local Indians and their first dogs.

From Lewiston, the Snake flows through eastern Washington to what is now Richland, where it joins the Columbia as it comes down south from Canada. Here, the Columbia flows west to the Pacific. This is the path that the corps followed.

The party reached the Columbia on October 16. Now, the group encountered the barren landscape of the Columbian Plain, in contrast to the wooded mountains they were leaving behind. They also encountered Indians who traveled by canoe, members of the "extended Nez Perce Nation" who lived on the river. These Indians had more horses than any tribe on the continent. But they ate horse meat only when threatened by starvation and seldom ate dogs. However, they were willing to sell dogs to the captains. The diet of these people was primarily deer and elk supplemented by large quantities of salmon and wapato roots. The men observed incredible numbers of salmon on the Columbia, and near its falls they found steelhead trout. Bernard DeVoto speculated that the men "became thoroughly bored by living on fish."[8]

After the party made its way though the Dalles, they encountered Indians with a culture and language different from any they had previously met—the Chinooks. During the first two days of November, the party made its way through the final barrier, the Cascades of the Columbia. The following day, moving downstream, the party came to Beacon Rock, the beginning of tidewater. They now were passing through another ecosystem, the thick rain forest of the Northwest Coast.

On November 2, the expedition passed the mouth of Sandy River. The night of the 3rd, the party camped on an island across from the mouth of the Williamette River near today's Vancouver, Washington. They used this site as a temporary base of operations. By the night of the 6th, however, it became obvious that their campsite was clearly unacceptable. Clark wrote, "we are all wet and disagreeable." So the party decided to seek other quarters. On the morning of November 7 there was fog. As it lifted, the expedition set off. By mid-afternoon the sky was clear. A shout went up. In his field notes, William Clark wrote this unforgettable line: "Ocian in view! O! the joy."

Clark's enthusiasm was slightly premature; what they were seeing was not the Pacific coast *per se* but the wide estuary of the Columbia, and signs of the tide. Nevertheless, a few days later Lewis and a small contingent, pushing ahead on an exploratory mission, reached the Pacific Ocean. The corps had arrived!

The party now was consuming mainly wapato roots and fish, which were staples in the lower Columbia area. By November 14, some of the men had found a much better site beyond Point Ellice, with game in the area. By November 17, the corps had moved its camp to this site, where the hunters could provide meat.

After getting better acquainted with the Chinooks, the men reacted negatively to them. The corps found that they had a penchant for thievery and exacted exorbitant prices for their food (probably the result of their considerable experience in bargaining with British sailors).[9]

Aware that the mountain snow would make the return east impossible for some months, the captains were faced with the question of where to spend the winter. While deer were available on the north side of the Columbia, elk were plentiful on the south. And the group, as a whole, preferred elk; they were fatter and much larger. The south side also was better for processing salt. And the party liked the Clatsop Indians, who lived on the south side, better than the Chinooks, on the north. Therefore, after much discussion, and finally a vote, it was decided to move to the south side. The captains chose a site which satisfied all of their requirements, including their desire for pure water, only thirty yards away at a spring. On December 7, Lewis guided the expedition to the site near today's Astoria, Oregon, and named their camp Fort Clatsop. The men set to work, some of them hunting, while others began cutting down trees for constructing their living quarters. The next day, Captain Clark selected a suitable place to set up a salt-making plant, where Seaside, Oregon, stands today.

The work went slowly. It seemed to rain most of the time, and the rain not only interfered with building their huts, it also made it impossible to preserve their food. Many of the injuries and other health problems previously noted still persisted. Nevertheless, the building project continued. Although the huts still lacked roofs, all of the men had moved in by Christmas Eve, and by December 30 the fort was completed.

On December 25, the men woke the captains with a volley, a shout, and a song. And, they exchanged modest presents. But the celebration did not last long. It was a wet and disagreeable day; Clark noted that there was "nothing to raise our spirits" since their liquor had run out July 4. Also, their dinner consisted of spoiled elk, spoiled fish, and a few roots.

The men had sex for diversion, as at previous times during the trip. But they paid the price for this activity by contracting venereal diseases. Lewis treated the men with mercurous chloride ointment. The party suffered from numerous other health problems while at Fort Clatsop, for many of their previous problems simply had not gone away. Other ailments, such as colds, fevers, and an influenza-like condition, may have been associated with the cold, wet weather and the confined quarters.

The captains believed that they had now accomplished the major objectives of the expedition. Coupled with the men's many health problems and low morale, this view was undoubtedly a key factor in their decision to depart from the fort earlier than planned. The party set out from Fort Clatsop on March 23, 1806, after a stay of about three and one-half months (Figure 5.2). That day, Clark introspectively had written, "[we] have lived as well as we had any right to expect, and we can say that we were never one day without three meals of some kind...either pore Elk meat or roots, notwithstanding the...rain which has fallen almost constantly...." Captain Clark obviously believed that, at least from the standpoint of quantity, the party had had sufficient food while at Fort Clatsop.

In departing, they must have looked much less impressive than they had at the beginning of the expedition in May 1804, or even upon departure from Fort Mandan in April 1805. They had left their camp at the mouth of the Wood River in a keelboat and two pirogues, carrying about eight tons of food along with other necessary supplies. Now, departing Fort Clatsop with thirty-one men, a toddler, and Sacagawea, in only five canoes, they had much less space for food and supplies, and far fewer items with which to barter. They had only a few items left for the purchase of more horses, if necessary, and half of the trip was still ahead of them.

Realistically, the captains knew that they would have to rely on the land for most of their food. On the return, the men were going to have to be more diligent in drying excess meat than they had been on the way out. Then, when hunting had been good and they had excess buffalo or fish, the men too often let it spoil rather than drying and making jerky out of it for future use. Instead, they rested. The Mandans had served as a poor example for the men in this regard; they rarely bothered to dry excess meat after a successful hunt.

By March 31, going up the Columbia, the party was approaching Sauvie Island, now a wildlife refuge near Portland, Oregon. The captains recognized this area as an excellent place for the men to hone their skills in hunting and drying meat. More important, they had to obtain enough food to last the party until it reached the Nez Perce lodges. During the six days they camped here, they obtained a good supply of meat and bartered for wapato roots from the natives.

They knew that, going through the plains to the Nez Perce camps at the base of the mountains, there would be no dogs, and no deer, pronghorn, or elk, either. To make matters worse, on April 1, some natives had told Lewis that food was very scarce above the falls, in part because the salmon run would not begin for another month. With this sobering news, the captains decided that, once they got into open country beyond the great rapids (the Dalles) they would go directly overland to the mountains. This situation further complicated matters because in order to do this they needed as many horses as possible, right now.

Clark went on ahead beyond the Dalles to set up an advance camp and begin buying horses. The Indians had plenty of them, but because horses were so indispensable to their lifestyle they did not want to sell any. Even so, after much effort and bargaining, Lewis and Clark were able to purchase ten horses. On April 24 the entire expedition marched overland, with nine horses carrying baggage and Private William Bratton riding on the remaining horse. A severe back condition prevented him from walking. That evening Lewis noted that most of the men were complaining of sore feet and legs; he himself had a very painful left ankle.

By the 27th, the party reached Chopunnish country, where the Wallawalla, relatives of the Nez Perce, lived. Soon, they encountered Chief Yelleppit, who invited the captains and the party to his village, promising them food and horses. But, like the Nez Perce, whom they had encountered the previous fall, they soon realized that for any food or other gifts they gave the party something was expected in return. And the Wallawalla drove a hard bargain. However, by the time they left these people on April 30, the men had succeeded in obtaining twenty-three horses. Further, the short cut to the Lolo Trail, suggested by Yelleppit, which took them across the base of the northern bend of the Snake, actually saved them about eighty miles. Thus, on balance, the captains were favorably impressed by the honesty and friendliness of these people.

Going almost due east across the arid plains of southeastern Washington, Clark wrote that on May 3 the party had made a scanty supper of their remaining dried meat and the last of their dogs. On May 4, they set out early and halted at the lodge of six families, where with much difficulty they purchased two lean dogs. They also obtained a few large cakes of half-cured bread made out of a root (probably "cows" or biscuit-root), which Lewis described as resembling the sweet potato, "with which we made some soope, and took breakfast."

Fortunately, that evening, the party met a band of Nez Perce led by Chief Tetoharsky, who had helped Twisted Hair in guiding them the previous fall. The captains bought some bread of cows roots and wood for fuel from these Indians, who offered to guide them to Twisted Hair's village. The next morning they set off early with their guides. Soon after their arrival, it became apparent that food was scarce at this village, too. They were unable to obtain any provisions at the first two lodges, and at the third they obtained only two dogs and a small amount of bread and dried roots. At the third lodge, Clark talked over a smoke with the principal person there. This Indian told him that his people had been so impressed with the medical care Clark had given them en route west that they would be interested in trading food in return for more medical care now. To the pragmatic Captain Clark, this sounded like a good idea. Lewis grudgingly assented, and for the next six weeks, while the men were waiting for the snow to melt up in the mountains, Captain Clark treated the people for a host of illnesses, which are detailed below in Chapter 6. In return, the Indians provided the party with much needed roots and dogs. Some of his own party required Clark's attention as well.

On May 7, while out reconnoitering on a high plain, the men caught sight of the Bitterroot Mountains and noted that their "spurs" [peaks] were still covered with snow. The Indians informed them that because of the heavy snows melting had been slow. In fact, the snow was still too deep to allow passage until about the first of June. This was bad news for the party. It meant they would have to wait at least three weeks longer before enjoying again that mouthwatering buffalo and other game so plentiful on the Missouri plains.

The good news was that beginning May 8 the men started to bag deer and other game. The foods which the Nez Perce were giving in return for medical care included camas, bread of cows, and an occasional colt or a quantity of dried fish. But their donations proved to be insufficient to sustain the men. It soon became necessary for each man to go out hunting every day to meet his individual food needs. Meanwhile, Twisted Hair, agonizingly deliberate, but ultimately true to his word, began to round up the horses which the men had left in his care. In the end, the party recovered twenty-one of its horses and about half the saddles. Meantime, Captain Clark devoted himself to caring for the sick.

On May 16, Sacagawea is described as gathering "a quantity of fennel roots which we find very palatable and nourishing food, the onion we also find in abundance and boil it with our meat." On May 18, Sacagawea is reported to have collected fennel again, this time "for the purpose of drying to eate on the Rocky mountains." Fennel is an herb with an anise-like taste which serves as a good garnish or flavor-enhancer, though not as a source of food.

Waiting for the snows in the mountains to melt enough for the party to proceed was extremely frustrating for the men. The expedition wanted to get to Mandan, then on to St. Louis before winter. On June 10, the party started out toward Weippe Prairie without guides, since the latter had deemed it too soon to proceed. After stopping at some quawmash fields to lay in some meat, the men resumed their journey on June 15. But after two days, they encountered so much snow that they were forced to retreat. They proceeded again, the next morning, June 17, to the top of a mountain, where they found themselves enveloped in even deeper snow—twelve to fifteen feet deep. With reluctance, they decided to return while their horses were still in good shape to an area where there would be enough grass.

On June 18, the captains sent Drouillard and Shannon back to the Nez Perce lodges to obtain a guide and then rejoin the party as soon as possible. The men did not return as expected, so the captains decided to return to the quawmash flats, where hunting would be better. Two days later, on the 23rd, Drouillard and Shannon returned, much to the party's relief. They had been delayed by their bargaining, which obviously had been successful since they now had three guides with them. And, better still, these guides had consented to accompany the party up to the falls of the Missouri in return for only two guns.

Early on the morning of June 24, the company started back toward the Bitterroots again. After reaching Weippe Prairie, they proceeded eastward, gathering up members of the party who had been hunting, enroute to Hungry Creek. On June 26 they moved on, recouping the baggage they had cached on the 16th and continuing their ascent. With the help of the experienced guides, on June 27 they reached Spring Mountain at 6,500 feet. Here, the snows had just melted so there was still very little grass for the horses. Moreover, the men had exhausted their meat supply.

On June 30th, after continuously coping with grass scarcity for the horses and food scarcity for the men, the hunters returned with six deer, which assured them of a bountiful supper. Just before sunset, the party arrived at the junction of a stream coming in from the west (Lolo Creek), which they had earlier named Travelers' Rest. The guides had saved the expedition; without their help, it is doubtful whether the party could have made its way safely across the Bitterroots. Also, thanks to the guides, they had been able to reach Travelers' Rest by July 1, in time to make some side-trips and still get back to St. Louis before the end of September.

Essentially, the plan now was for Clark to go down the Jefferson River and on to Three Forks, where he would cross over to the Yellowstone Valley and proceed down the Yellowstone River to its juncture with the Missouri. Meanwhile, Lewis would follow the Nez Perce trail to the Great Falls, then go down the Missouri to the mouth of the Marias River. Next, he would follow the Marias to its source in an effort to learn whether any of its branches extended at least to fifty degrees north. Such information would be invaluable to President Jefferson since furs from Canada could legitimately be transported to American ports from any navigable affluent so situated. This goal realized, Lewis and his party would continue down the Missouri to the mouth of the Yellowstone and reunite with Clark and his party about the 12th of August.

Lewis and Clark knew that the Marias area was Blackfeet country. But they did not seem to realize what a threat this Indian tribe could pose for Lewis and his small group of men if they met up with them going up the Marias River. In fact, this potentially was the most dangerous mission on the entire homeward journey.

On the morning of July 3, the captains and the men said goodbye and went their separate ways. Clark with his party, embarking on his planned trip, went southward. At the same time, Lewis and nine men, with five Nez Perce guides and seventeen horses, set out northward down the Bitterroot River. Crossing the river by raft at ten miles, they continued eastward along today's Clark Fork River to within a couple of miles of today's Missoula, Montana. Here, they camped and feasted on the deer which the hunters had brought in.

Next day, July 4, their Nez Perce guides left them to go home, and Lewis's party proceeded eastward on their own. They had embarked on a trek that following the Nez Perce trail, took them over the Divide, then down into buffalo country and on to the Missouri. Then they followed the Missouri, going northeast, to the mouth of the Marias River. During this time, deer were plentiful, followed later by large numbers of buffalo, elk, and bear. From the buffalo skins the men made bull boats for use on the Missouri.

On July 16, they began to follow the Marias River upstream until the afternoon of July 23 where the river forked into two branches, now called Cut Bank Creek, coming in from the north, and Two Medicine River, coming in from the south. Following the Cut Bank fork, near today's Glacier National Park, Lewis noted that it came out of the mountain from the southwest, *not* from the north! Realizing that he had reached the Cut Bank's northernmost point, he "lost hope of the water of this river extending to N Latitude 50 degrees."

En route back to the Missouri, the men became involved in a fracas with a party of Piegan Indians, one of the three Blackfeet groups. Reubin Field mortally stabbed one of the Indians with his knife, and Lewis shot another in the belly. As the Piegans scattered, Lewis and his men hurriedly saddled their horses and embarked on a forced march to the mouth of the Marias. They needed to get away as quickly as possible, of course, but they also wanted to meet Sergeant Ordway and his canoe party, who would be coming down from the falls soon. That group needed to be alerted to the impending arrival of the Blackfeet. They finally stopped for the night at 2:00 a.m., having been up since 3:30 a.m. the previous day. On July 28 Lewis woke at dawn "so soar he could scarcely stand." The men felt the same. But Lewis galvanized them into action, reminding them of the life-or-death situation they and Ordway's group were in. They were soon underway and reached the Missouri just in time to meet Ordway and his men as they arrived. There would have been a brief exchange of greetings while Lewis explained their need for haste. But the journals merely note that they quickly transferred the baggage from the horses to the canoes. Presumably, the horses were turned loose at this point. After descending the river for about fifteen miles, and assuming that they had rid themselves of the Blackfeet, the men made camp.

Lewis's party met Clark's near the mouth of the Yellowstone on August 12. The next day, the united expedition took off for the Mandan villages, where the Mandans feted them for three days. The Mandans were "extreamly pleased to See us," Clark wrote. On August 17, the men started on the home stretch to St. Louis, leaving Sacagawea, Charbonneau, and their little son with the Mandans.

Back on the Missouri, it was downriver all the way, both literally and figuratively. They were making unexpectedly good time for several reasons. Now, they were navigating pirogues and canoes rather than the clumsy, heavy barge. They had been coming upstream in 1804; now, they were going downstream, the current was strong, and the oarsmen, anxious to get home, applied themselves diligently. Finally, buffalo, elk, and deer abounded, along with plums—which was fortunate because their food stores by now were completely exhausted.

By September 18, the party was within 150 miles of the settlements. They still had their rifles and there was game in the neighborhood, but the frequent passage of traders' boats had caused the deer and bear to move back from the river. So, to obtain meat, the hunters would have had to go out on foot, which would have delayed the party considerably. Instead, considering their eagerness to get home, they allayed their hunger by eating "poppaws" (plums), which could be gathered quickly near shore.

On September 20, they were coming into home country. Putting in at La Charrette, Missouri, the men fired three rounds, which were returned by three rounds from five trading boats on the river bank. The citizens rushed to them, delighted by their safe return. On the 21st, the scene was repeated at St. Charles (now a suburb of St. Louis). The expedition was officially completed September 22 when they arrived at Fort Belle Fontaine, a few miles up the Missouri. Here they were honored by a salute of guns and a hearty welcome.

Chapter 6
Dietary and Health Assessment

The captains had been very careful in their choice of recruits. They both believed that the judicious selection of appropriate men was critical to the success of their undertaking.[1] On June 19, 1803, in a letter to Clark, Lewis had indicated that he was "looking for some good hunters, stout, healthy, unmarried men, accustomed to the woods, and capable of bearing bodily fatigue in a pretty considerable degree." He had added that "the soldiers that will most probably answer this expedition best will be found in some of the companies stationed at Massac, Kaskaskias, & Illinois...."[2] It turned out that, since the captains had far more applicants than they could accept, they could afford to be selective. John Colter and George Shannon had been conditionally chosen by Captain Lewis in Pittsburgh in late August 1803 and had accompanied him during the entire trip down the Ohio. Meanwhile Clark had tentatively picked Charles Floyd, Nathaniel Pryor, William Bratton, Reubin Field, Joseph Field, George Gibson, and John Shields. Later, all of these men were officially accepted, along with others from the area. These men were all young, ranging in age from sixteen (George Shannon) to thirty-four (John Shields).

It appears that there are no organized data available regarding the heights and weights of the men in the Lewis and Clark party. However, it is known that, by the time of the American Revolution, native-born white males ages thirty-four to thirty-five (presumably soldiers) averaged 68.1 inches. This value is virtually identical with heights in the United States Army during World War II[3]—a stature which would suggest a fairly high level of nutrition. From these data one can surmise that members of the Lewis and Clark party also averaged about five-feet-eight inches in height and that they, too, had a reasonably good nutritional history. In fact, having passed the captains' scrutiny, they must have been generally healthy.

Nonetheless, assuming that their diets were typical of those consumed during the early years of the Republic, they undoubtedly had the same deficits noted in Table 1.2 , column 2. Therefore, by today's nutritional standards their diets fell short of the ideal.

The corps arrived at Camp Dubois on December 12, 1803. On May 14, 1803, after five months, they were ready to depart up the Missouri and formally begin the expedition. Table 6.1, column 1, evaluates their dietary adequacy at the end of this time, as well as at subsequent key points during the expedition. These assessments have been made using information obtained from the journals regarding the party's food consumption.

At Camp Dubois, the men undoubtedly had enjoyed a more dependable and uniform diet than prior to enlistment. While at their winter camp, the men also had been able to obtain rations from the U.S. Army commissaries and contractors on the Mississippi, particularly the post (with its commissary) at St. Louis. Thus, they could save on their stores of food, including the portable soup which Captain Lewis had purchased and brought on the barge from Pittsburgh. They had plenty of staple foods, such as pork, biscuit, flour, various meals, and lard. And they had been obtaining quite a bit of game by hunting during the winter and drinking river water. Therefore, their intake of protein, carbohydrates, and fats,

Table 6.1–Dietary Adequacy of the Lewis and Clark Party, 1805-1806

NUTRIENT	1804 MAY	1805 APRIL	1805 AUGUST	1805 OCTOBER	1806 MARCH	1806 SEPTEMBER
Water (fluids)	+	+	—	-	+	+
Fiber	-	-	-	-	-	-
Total Calories	+	+	(+)	-	+	(+)
Carbohydrate	+	+	+	-	+	(+)
Fat	+	+	+++	-	+	+
Protein	+	++	(+++)	-	++	+
Vitamins						
Folic Acid	-	-	—	—	-	-
Niacin	+	+	+	-	+	+
Riboflavin	(+)	(+)	-	—	(+)	-
Thiamin	+	+	+	-	(+)	(+)
Vit. B12	+	(+)	+	-	+	(+)
Vitamin C	-	-	—	—	—	-
Vitamin A (or carotene)	-	(+)	-	-	(+)	-
Vitamin D	-	-	-	-	(+)	-
Vitamin E	-	-	-	-	-	-
Minerals						
Calcium	-	-	—	—	-	-
Magnesium	+	(+)	-	-	(+)	-
Phosphorus	+	+	+	-	+	+
Potassium	+	+	+	-	+	+
Sodium	+	+	+	-	+	+
Iodine	-	-	-	-	+	-
Iron	+	+	+	-	+	(+)
Copper	+	+	+	-	+	+
Manganese	+	+	+	-	(+)	(+)
Zinc	+	+	+	-	+	+

as well as calories and fluids, should have been adequate. Their intake of the vitamins and minerals contained in these foods should have been adequate as well: niacin, thiamin, vitamin B12, magnesium, phosphorus, potassium, sodium, iron, copper, manganese and zinc. However, in the rare instances where the journals report the party's obtaining milk it seems to have been obtained in very small quantity. It must have been intended for use in coffee or tea, and then perhaps only by the captains. No tea and only fifty pounds of coffee appear on their list of provisions (Table 5.1). Eggs, vegetables, and fruits also seem to have been rarely eaten at Camp Dubois. Since their diets had been lacking in milk, fish, eggs, fruits and vegetables, they were lacking in fiber, folic acid, riboflavin (borderline), vitamins C, A, D, E, and the minerals calcium and iodine, as seen in Table 6.1, column 1, for May 1804.

Despite their dietary deficits, from comments in the journals regarding the men soon after they were recruited one can assume that the men were generally healthy, at least by the standards of the early nineteenth-century. During the winter, there are few entries made by Clark regarding the health of the men.[4] However, Captain Clark mentions his own health problems quite frequently. Despite them, he seemed able to carry out his duties. During the last weeks prior to the party's departure in May, there were frequent visits to

Camp Dubois by a Dr. Catlett, presumably associated with the post at St. Louis, which were never really explained. He may have been coming out to treat possible ailments of the party and/or to give all of the men check-ups prior to their departure up the Missouri. But the journals shed little light on this matter.

Most of the men had been recruited from the lower Ohio River and Mississippi valleys, where malaria was endemic. Thus, it is likely that most, if not all, of the men had malaria and that they experienced periodic recurrences of fever and ague. However, the only case of malaria formally recorded in the journals was by Lewis in reference to himself. He described his bout with fever and ague while going down the Ohio, which began just as the party left Fort Massac on November 13, 1803. The lack of entries regarding malaria attacks involving other members of the party may be due to their being viewed as too commonplace to warrant mention. At least some of the vaguely described cases of sickness reported in the journals could have been due to malaria attacks. Venereal disease also was a common affliction among the men. It, too, was under-reported throughout the trip, probably because it occurred so frequently among military personnel during this era.

On May 14, 1804, the corps departed from Camp Dubois and moved up the Missouri. Until they reached Mandan country, the health of the party was quite good, with one major exception. On August 20, 1804, Sergeant Charles Floyd died near present Sioux City, Iowa, of a burst appendix and subsequent peritonitis. Even if a surgeon had been present, nothing could have been done for him since the technique for the removal of a diseased appendix was not developed until many years later.[5]

By mid-October, they had arrived in Mandan country where they spent the winter. Upon their arrival, the party observed that the Indians here raised maize or Indian corn, beans, potatoes, pumpkins, watermelons, squashes and a unique species of tobacco. At this time of year, the Mandans were harvesting their gardens, and they gave the men large quantities of squash and other yellow vegetables. It soon became apparent that meat (particularly buffalo) was the mainstay of the Mandans' diet during winter. The corps learned that, during the summer, or when game was scarce in the winter, these Indians relied on their horticultural products (especially corn, beans, and squashes) for food.

The men went out hunting frequently while at Fort Mandan—singly, in small groups, or as a large party, usually along with the Mandans. Hunting in a large group with the Indians was thought to be safer, in case of an attack by the Sioux. It also was more likely to result in larger amounts of game. On February 12, for example, Lewis reported that hunting as a large party had resulted in as many as forty deer and sixteen elk. However, most of the animals by this time of the winter were so thin from lack of food that they were unfit for consumption.

Upon their arrival, the Mandans had welcomed them with gifts of food without obvious expectations of reciprocation. Soon after, it became apparent that the Indians did expect something in return. On November 12, Big White, the principal chief of the lower village, had his wife carry into camp 100 bushels of corn. In return, the captains gave some small presents to his wife and child, including a small axe, with which she "was much pleased." From then on, a pattern of reciprocation seemed to evolve, whereby the Indians traded food, such as corn, pumpkin, or pemmican, for axes or other metal utensils, or for the repair of such items. They valued these articles very much. By February 19, Clark wrote, "Our Smiths are much engaged mending and making Axes for the Indians for which we get Corn." Later, having noted that the Lewis and Clark party was making preparations to depart, the Indians began to come with increasing frequency, hoping to trade corn for axes while the corps still remained at Mandan. On March 13, Clark noted, "Maney [Indians] here today...all anxiety for war axes...the Smiths have not an hour Idle time to Spear...."

In addition to their other duties, the captains frequently attended to various health needs while at Fort Mandan. They treated not only members of the corps (including themselves) but the Indians, the interpreters, and their families.

Incipient problems regarding sex and venereal disease became evident as soon as they arrived in Mandan country. Going up the Missouri, the men had been offered sexual favors by both the Sioux and the Arikara. And, upon reaching Mandan country, these sexual overtures continued. By January 14, Clark noted, "Several men with the Venereal cought from the Mandan women." By March 31, his journal entry reflected guarded concern. He described the men as "Generally healthy, except Venerials Complaints which is verry Common amongst the natives and the men Catch it from them."

Both Captain Clark and John Shields suffered from rheumatism while at Mandan. There are several entries regarding members of the party having bad colds. Sergeant Pryor dislocated his shoulder in taking down the mast. Clark reported that the captains made four trials before they replaced it. Many people had to be treated for frost bite—members of the party, including York and Charbonneau, as well as the Indians. In one case, despite treatment (usually repetitive soaking in cold water), a little Indian boy's toes eventually had to be sawed off. There are other entries describing Captain Clark and the interpreter, René Jesseaume, as being unwell. On two occasions, Jesseaume was given "a dost of salts."

On December 21 an Indian woman brought a child with an abscess and offered as much corn as she could carry "for some Medison." On the 7th of March another sick Indian child was brought in, to whom Clark gave some Rush's pills.

On January 31 Clark wrote, "George Drewyer taken with the Pleurisy last evening. Bled & gave him Some Sage tea, this morning he is much better." There were numerous injuries incurred by working with axes; two men hurt their hips very much by falling down (presumably on the ice).

There was one childbirth on the journey. On February 11, 1805, Captain Lewis attended Sacagawea at the birth of her firstborn, a son.

As the winter of 1804-05 ended at Fort Mandan, with the help of the Indians the men had survived. Without their assistance in hunting, and gifts of corn and other dried vegetables when game was scarce, the outcome might have been much less sanguine. During their stay with the Mandans, the captains had been kept quite occupied taking care of the health needs of themselves and their neighbors. But the corps emerged from the winter in relatively good health.

By April 1805, the men were making preparation to resume their journey westward. Table 6.1, column 2, evaluates their dietary adequacy at this time, as well as at subsequent key points during the expedition. These assessments have been made using information obtained from the journals regarding the party's food consumption.

Except for George Shannon, none of the party, as of April 1805, had suffered from a serious lack of food *per se*. Total calorie intake probably had been adequate but not excessive. Since the group had been highly active, it is doubtful that any of the men had gained weight during the past months. The men had sufficient carbohydrate, fat, and protein. In fact, protein intake occasionally had been excessive because of high meat consumption—

several pounds per day at times. Despite their intake of salt pork, fat intake probably had not been excessive, considering the men's activity level. Also, most of the game obtained had been relatively lean, especially as the winter wore on.

However, there had been some nutrient deficiencies. Since leaving St. Louis, the staple of their diet had been meat. Therefore, none of the men were lacking in protein, or the vitamins and minerals strongly associated with meat: thiamine, niacin, vitamin B-12, potassium, sodium, iron, and zinc. Since much of their food was heavily salted, their sodium intake had to have been high. But, considering their active lives and associated perspiration (especially the previous summer, going up the Missouri), high sodium should not have posed a problem. Magnesium probably was borderline in adequacy because of lack of green vegetables and the use of "hulled grain."

Although not reflected in Table 6.1, column 2, the fluid intake probably had been inadequate during the summer of 1804, and their diet and lifestyle had exacerbated this situation. For example, their diet was fairly salty, they perspired a great deal, and they drank whiskey daily, all of which would contribute to dehydration.

After embarking on their expedition in May 1804 there was absolutely no reference to milk, cheese, or eggs. So, upon reaching Mandan, with a diet lacking in dairy products, eggs, and vegetables for over a year, their intakes of vitamins A, D, folic acid and calcium also had been very low. Riboflavin intake has been borderline. A deficiency of this vitamin manifests itself quickly, which explains, in part, the group's chronic problem of sore eyes, reported in the journals. Lack of vitamin C can also result in sore eyes. Folic acid intake probably was low, also, because of a lack of sufficient green vegetables and legumes, putting the men at risk for megaloblastic anemia. Lack of dairy products and eggs can also result in low vitamin A and D intakes. However, overt symptoms of deficiency for either of these vitamins probably had not yet occurred for the following reasons. With respect to vitamin A, since most people who are reasonably well-nourished have about a year's store of vitamin A in their livers, and assuming that the men all were in fairly good nutritional status when they were inducted, they could rely on their vitamin A stores until about the end of October 1804. But, by that time, on these diets their stores would be getting low. Coincidentally, the party reached Mandan country by that very time (October 26, 1804). And, since this also happened to be the time of year when the Indians were harvesting their gardens, they gave the corps large quantities of squash and other yellow vegetables. These vegetables are very high in carotene, which is easily converted in the body to vitamin A. Thus, their supply of this vitamin probably was adequate. With virtually no consumption of milk, cheese, and eggs, their intake of vitamin D *per se* had to be low, also. However, many foods contain ergosterol and 7-dehydrocholesterol, which can be converted to vitamin D in the skin under the influence of sunlight. And these outdoorsmen had been having plenty of exposure to sunlight. So it is doubtful that the men were actually suffering from vitamin D deficiency. Body stores of vitamin E were probably low because of the lack of vegetable oils and the fact that meat is low in this vitamin.

With the scarcity of dairy products, green leafy vegetables, and soybeans, the men had to be lacking in the mineral calcium. But this lack would not pose an immediate problem for this reason: the body can leach whatever calcium it needs from the bones and other body stores in order to maintain the necessary level of calcium in the blood. Thus, one would not expect any overt symptoms from calcium deficiency yet. A mild osteoporosis could have begun. But, as noted earlier, these were all young men, ranging in age now from about eighteen for George Shannon, to thirty-six for John Shields. Within this youthful group one would not expect to see outward signs of osteoporosis yet.

Undoubtedly the men were lacking in vitamin C. For several weeks after leaving Camp Dubois they had access to various seasonal berries and other fruit high in vitamin C. But one gets the impression that these fruits did not constitute a substantial component of their diets. So, especially since little vitamin C is stored in the body, it can be assumed that most of the men were suffering from vitamin C deficiency by now. In addition, they would have been under stress, which increased the excretion of this and other nutrients, resulting in a lessened immune response. This combination of factors could explain the frequent occurrence of sore eyes, boils, and slow wound healing.

The diets of the men had been somewhat lacking in iodine thus far on the trip. And they may well have started out with somewhat depleted body stores of this mineral, since goiter was common in the Ohio River Valley from which many of the group had come. Although their diet had been high in salt, it still could have been low in iodine, since iodized salt did not become available to consumers until 1924. They had caught some freshwater fish en route, but its iodine content does not compare with that of saltwater fish.

There were other related health problems. They definitely had a low fiber intake, resulting in frequent complaints of constipation. Captain Clark wrote frequently about his gastrointestinal problems. Captain Lewis treated him with various "fesics" and other potions. Many of the men had suffered thus far from flu and dysentery, which could have been caused by the river water, polluted by run-off from the river bank. There is no record of their ever having boiled it. This run-off included fragments of decaying dead buffalo and other animal carcasses, fecal material of both animal and human origin, plus garbage thrown in by passing traders and local Indians. Under such circumstances, one can empathize with a rebellious member of the party, somewhat censured by the others, for his boasting that he "never drank water." (However, he must have drunk enough fluid to survive.)

Another factor that added to their health problems was the captains' penchant for bleeding the men on the slightest pretext, a common medical practice during this era. Unfortunately, blood-letting can be dangerously weakening, usually exacerbating rather than curing an illness.

Lewis was fond of using some of the plant potions recommended by his mother, including walnut bark, which Gary Moulton describes as being strongly emetic and also a mild purgative.[6] Lewis's stockpile of medicines included some compounds that were high in arsenic and mercury, in common use during that era. Thus, it is possible that the recovery of these men from their occasional ailments may have occurred at times in spite of the treatments received rather than because of them.

The day of departure from Fort Mandan was an exciting one for the party. The men were enthusiastic—especially Lewis. Earlier this day, he had written to President Jefferson: "Since our arrival at this place we have subsisted on meat, with which our guns have supplied us amply, and have thus been enabled to reserve the parched meal, portable soup, and a considerable portion of pork and flour, which we had intended for the more difficult parts of our voyage. If the Indian information can be credited, the vast quantity of game with which the country (to the west) abound...leaves us but little to apprehend from the want of food....As to myself...I never enjoyed a more perfect state of good health, than I have since I commenced our voyage. My...friend and companion, Capt. Clark, has also enjoyed good health generally. At this moment, every individual of the party are in good health, and excellent sperits...and anxious to proceed; not a whisper of discontent or murmur is to be heard among them;...with such men I have every thing to hope, and but little to fear."[7] One wonders whether Lewis really felt this confident about the upcoming journey. These remarks may simply have been intended to impress his superior. Or these comments could have reflected one of Lewis's reputedly manic moods. He seemed much more sanguine than the situation at that time warranted. After all, the men had been experiencing more than a few problems. And the likelihood of their encountering even more, going westward, was great. The party had experienced some nutrition and health problems while at Fort Mandan, ignored completely in the letter to Jefferson. And, of the many challenges facing the party, obtaining proper nutrition and maintaining the health of the men were of paramount importance.

Notably, although the captains had made meticulous notes of the food and other articles to be loaded on their vessels before leaving St. Louis, no similar lists seem to have been made prior to leaving Mandan. From Lewis's letter to Jefferson, just cited, we learn that they still had some stores of non-perishable food. But, at best, it could serve only as a supplement to the meat and other food they would have to obtain by daily hunting and foraging.

After leaving Fort Mandan on April 7, the captains do not mention food until April 9, when Lewis reported halting for dinner and that Sacagawea had collected a good quantity of wild artichokes for the men that day. On May 8, en route to the Musselshell, she also gathered some wild licorice root and the white apple.

The party had found game to be scarce during the first ten days after leaving Fort Mandan, probably because of heavy local hunting by the Hidatsa and Assiniboin Indians.[8] However, they soon began to see signs of the long-awaited game. On April 14 Clark killed the party's first buffalo. Since it was thin from the harsh winter, they kept only its marrow bones and a small amount of meat. This was the first of numerous references made to the party's consumption of bone marrow along the way. It was not long before Clark reported seeing large numbers of buffalo, elk, antelope, and deer. As soon as grass became more plentiful, and game became fatter, the men began to render quantities of fat from butchered animals for cooking and other uses.

These utopian conditions continued until they reached the mouth of the Musselshell River, May 20. Here, there was very little grass and much less game. As they proceeded, the game available varied with the changing ecosystems. Their diet consisted mainly of meat in large quantities, which served to sustain them as they travelled up the Missouri.

Between June 16 and July 14, 1805, while most of the men were involved in portaging around the Great Falls, others were hunting or fishing to obtain food for the party. On June 11, Goodrich, the fisherman of the group, caught several dozen fish—gold eye and cutthroat trout.

The general health of the group seemed to be quite good for about two months after leaving Fort Mandan. But then the rigors of the trip, deficiencies in the diet, occasional bleedings, and other factors began to take their toll. On June 3 at the Marias River, Lewis noted that the men "...have fallen off considerably..." (i.e., lost weight). Some days later, he felt very unwell himself. So he took a portion of salts from which he felt much relief that evening. But the next day Lewis wrote that he was taken with such violent pain in the intestines that he was unable to partake of the evening meal. He later developed a high fever. Miraculously, after drinking some tea that he had made by boiling chokecherry twigs in water, he was relieved of all symptoms, including fever, by night. Lewis had learned how to prepare these "decoctions" or "simples" from his herbalist mother.[6]

The journals note that at this time he and others of the party (including Clark) were taking salts, including Rush's pills, for constipation and/or other digestive complaints.

On June 10, Clark had written, "...Sacahgawea our Indian woman very sick...I blead her." On June 14, Clark described her condition as "somewhat dangerous." Next day, he reported, "I gave her the bark and apply it externally to her region which revived her much...." By June 19, Lewis wrote that she was feeling much better, but her husband allowed her to go out and gather "a considerable quantity of the white apples of which she eat heartily in their raw state...that she complained very much and her fever returned." He then gave her "broken doses of diluted nitre...and at 10 p.m. 30 drops of laudnum which gave her a tolerable nights rest." This illness, which included a fever, continued about ten days, during which time both Clark and Lewis administered to her. They continued to give her Peruvian bark tea and an opium preparation (laudanum), and she recovered.

On June 14, Clark reported two men with tooth ache and six men with tumors, one of whom also had a slight fever. Many seemed to be experiencing dehydration and heat exhaustion, exacerbated by the tremendous exertion required by the portaging efforts. On June 26, Whitehouse became "extremely ill" from heat exhaustion, followed by drinking too much water upon his arrival at camp. Lewis reported that he "therefore bled him plentifully from which he felt great relief." Meanwhile, at the lower camp, Captain Clark gave Sergeant Pryor a dose of salts.

On July 15, having made a successful portage around the Great Falls, the men started out in search of the source of the Missouri. They also were looking for the Shoshones, who thus far had evaded them. The party now proceeded with eight canoes, which had been loaded with their belongings and supplies. The latter included about 600 pounds of dried meat, considerable "grease," and several dozen dried trout.

Captain Clark had indicated in his journal entry of July 13 that he wished this dried meat (and presumably some of the grease) to be used for the making of pemmican. Shortly after their departure, on several days Clark reported seeing shrubs, many with berries. This was fortuitous, since berries are also usually used in making this food product. They included chokecherries, red berries, gooseberries, and various kinds of currants. Although there is no mention of the men's having gathered them, they certainly must have availed themselves of these berries for making pemmican.

On July 19, the party encamped at a spot which Captain Lewis called the "gates of the rocky mountains." On July 22, while walking on shore, Lewis saw "...great quantities of a small onion about the size of a musquit ball..." which were "...white crisp and well flavored...." He gathered about a half bushel of them; then, having halted the party, the men also gathered considerable quantities of these onions. On July 25, Clark noted that he with a party of four men (Frazer, Joseph and Reubin Field, and Charbonneau) went on ahead a few miles to the Three Forks of the Missouri. Next day, leaving Charbonneau (who had a bad ankle) and another man (who had sore feet) to rest, Clark and the two other men proceeded to the top of a mountain which afforded a good view of the Three Forks. They found a spring of cold water in the mountains, from which they drank freely. It was a scorching day. Later Clark reported that he felt very unwell. On July 27, Lewis (who by now had arrived with the rest of the party) wrote that Captain Clark had a high fever, was feeling bilious, and was constipated. Whereupon, Lewis prevailed on him to take a dozen of Rush's pills, his favorite remedy for this ailment. Clark's entry for that same day indicates that he actually settled for taking only five. According to Ronald Loge, M.D., "a person presenting now with these symptoms during the summer season in southwestern Montana would usually be suffering from Colorado tick fever. This viral infection...is endemic today in the Three Forks area."[9]

July 31 marked a low point for Lewis, as well as for the entire party. He wrote that nothing was killed that day, and that their fresh meat "is out." He complained about the men: "...when we have a plenty of fresh meat I find it impossible to make the men take any care of it, or use it with the least frugality, tho' I expect that necessity will shortly teach them this art."

On that same day, Lewis went on to say, "We have a lame crew just now, two with tumors or bad boils on various parts of them, one with a bad stone bruise, one with his arm accidentally dislocated but fortunately well replaced, and a fifth [Sergeant Gass] has streigned his back by slipping and falling backwards on the gunwall of the canoe." A few days later, Captain Clark developed a tumor on his ankle, and on August 5 Drouillard sprained a finger and badly injured one leg in a fall.

By early August 1805 the corps had been en route from Fort Mandan about four months. From early April to July 15, although the men had been consuming extremely large quantities of meat, their health had deteriorated greatly. At the same time, the party's dietary lacks had worsened considerably since leaving Fort Mandan (Table 6.1, column 3, August 1805). All of the men were tired. Without a doubt, the heat and the exhaustion experienced during portaging were debilitating. And the group undoubtedly was suffering added stress from the entire expedition at this point.

As on their voyage the previous year from St. Louis to Mandan, the men had been consuming more than enough protein and fat and supposedly adequate calories. But they had many other dietary deficiencies. Essentially, they were the same lacks which they had after the first leg of the journey (Table 6.1, column 2, April 1805). But, as the length and arduousness of their journey increased, their dietary deficits became more pronounced. Dehydration had become a serious problem, mainly because of the extended period of hot weather and the party's strenuous exertions. In addition, their drinking water frequently had been polluted by run-off from the river bank. Both inadequate fluid and fiber had contributed to their frequent bouts of constipation. And, despite a reasonable calorie intake, the men had lost weight, as Lewis reported earlier. This weight loss undoubtedly was caused by the increased energy expenditures evoked by the increased exertion of the portaging, exacerbated by their going uphill. In addition, stress itself results in increased excretion of all the nutrients, plus lowered immunity. With their high level of activity, the men probably had been expending well over 5,000 kilocalories daily during the portaging period. Thus, their calorie needs were high also. But the men had been meeting these needs by consuming too much protein and fat (in the form of meat), placing increased demands on the gastrointestinal system, liver and kidneys (see Chapter 7). Such strains could explain the frequently reported complaints of "biliousness." On the positive side, they would have had good intakes of the vitamins and minerals found in meat: thiamine, niacin, vitamin B-12, potassium, sodium, iron, and zinc. But their intakes of riboflavin, folic acid, and vitamins C, A, D, and E had been low, as well as the minerals magnesium and calcium. Iodine intake probably was borderline (Table 6.1, column 3, August 1805). Their dietary deficits were due to the lack of dairy products, eggs, sea food, whole grains, fruits and vegetables. The occasional consumption of artichokes, wild onions, white apples, and wild licorice added much needed variety to their diets, but it had not provided an adequate vegetable and fruit intake. Their lowered nutritional status contributed in various degrees to most of their health problems. Deficiencies of riboflavin and vitamin C can develop quickly and probably were the prime cause of the men's sore eyes, as well as the rashes, boils (sometimes called tumors), and slow wound healing (typical of scurvy). Pricks from the prickly pear cactus and other brush, along with other abrasions that they frequently incurred, undoubtedly provided opportunities for staphylococcus and other infections to develop. And they had no antibiotics or other really effective medications for treatment. Some of the fevers that the men experienced probably were caused by recurrent bouts of malaria, since most of them had come from areas where that disease was endemic. In addition, the blood-letting that the captains favored had a weakening effect, potentially causing anemia, as well as a dehydrating effect—ultimately doing more harm than good. It is amazing how well the sick recovered under the circumstances.

Sacagawea's illness and treatment have attracted the interest of many students of the Lewis and Clark Expedition. Dr. Drake W. Will and other medical experts have nearly agreed that she was suffering from pelvic inflammatory disease (P.I.D.).[10] According to Dr. Eldon Chuinard, her history as a captive-slave among the diseased and licentious Hidatsa lend probability to this diagnosis; he stated that the disease probably was gonorrheal in nature.[11] Bruce C. Paton, M.D., has pointed out that the captains' bleeding and purging of Sacagawea undoubtedly weakened and dehydrated her, which upset the electrolyte balance of her blood as well. Lewis wisely directed that she be given water from a nearby mineral spring to drink, which could very well have corrected her electrolyte disturbance.[12] Howard J. Beard, M.D., lauded the care given Sacagawea by the captains; he described the medical observations as exceptional and their bedside notes as being extraordinary.[13]

The picture that was presented to the corps, as they contemplated the remaining (and actually most challenging) obstacle on their journey to the Pacific, was gloomy indeed. They now needed to pass over the Rocky Mountains to some navigable tributary of the Columbia River. But the truth was that the men really did not feel very well. Nevertheless, they proceeded on.

At the Three Forks area, getting ready to go over the Divide, the party found themselves in a dry, rugged ecosystem. The men went out hunting every day, but there was little food to be had in this area, except grouse and some roots and berries. And the party's food staples had become very low. In mid-August, while Lewis and three of the men were on their exploratory mission over the Divide, they failed to get any game. That evening, the only food they had left was a pound of flour, which they stirred into boiling water to make a gruel for their supper. It was fortunate that the party's actual crossing of the Divide took only one day—August 26. The food problem attendant with this journey had been magnified immensely by the fact that Chief Cameahwait, whom Lewis had met while reconnoitering on the other side of the Divide, had brought his entire band of Indians over with him, when he crossed the Lemhi Pass to escort the corps back over the Divide.

Although the crossing of the Divide took only one day, the preparations preceding it, coupled with the party's stay at the Shoshone camp on the Lemhi River afterward, consumed a period of twenty-three days (August 9-31, 1805).

Figure 6.1 Death Camas and Blue Camas growing together. *Image by Drs. Nancy J. and Robert D. Turner.*

Figure 6.2 Camas roots (bulbs). *Image by Drs. Nancy J. and Robert D. Turner.*

Certainly the men had gone a little hungry during this period. What they did not know was that they soon would face much more severe food scarcity. The party left Cameahwait's camp on the Lemhi River on September 1, 1805, to go over the Bitterroots. They had no idea that this enterprise in its entirety would consume thirty-six days, until October 6.

By September 3, Captain Clark noted that there was "but little to eate." Nothing but grouse, here, either. The party consumed the last of its salt pork that day. But, on September 4, at the Bitterroot River, it met a band of friendly Salish Indians who gave them some of their berries and roots. Most likely, the latter were bitterroots. As implied by their name, these roots have a bitter taste, but are not poisonous, and were widely used by the Indians in these mountains. However, the men did not like the bitterroots. Not surprisingly, then, there is no record of their ever foraging for them. Indeed, they seem not to have looked for roots of any kind during this trip. Their behavior perhaps is best explained by the Optimal Foraging Theory, developed by D. R. Yesner.[14] Put simply, it states that people will tend to invest their energies preferentially on obtaining foods of maximum nutrient density.[15] Obviously, it made sense for the Lewis and Clark party to focus on securing game, rather than roots, when food was a limiting factor. Bitterroots were the first of three root staples that the men would encounter west of the Divide. Later, proceeding west, they would be introduced to camas and wapato roots.

On September 6, the party set off down the Bitterroot River going north. That night, they had nothing to eat but two grouse and some berries, divided among thirty-three people. The captains were out of flour and had in their larder only a little corn and the portable soup Lewis had purchased in Philadelphia, to be used only in emergencies.

Finally, by September 9, they were about to cross the Bitterroots. That night, the men camped at Travelers' Rest, where Captain Lewis decided to rest the horses for a day. On the morning of the 10th, he sent out all the hunters for meat, hoping to replenish their supply before going over the mountains.

On September 11, they finally got started up Lolo Pass, over the Bitterroots. During the next few days, the food situation became so serious that the men were forced to kill their three colts, one at a time, for food.

September 16 was the worst day the expedition had experienced so far. A big snowfall piled up snow from six to eight inches deep, making it almost impossible to find the trail. They had now killed the last of the colts. Both the horses and the party were near starvation. The party had reached an emotional and physical nadir. The food supply was all but gone. Lewis and Clark realized that they, as well as the men, were at a breaking point. The captains discussed their alternatives. They finally decided that Clark would go on ahead with six hunters to level country to hunt for food to send back to the party. On September 18, Captain Clark and his group started out; Lewis and the others were to follow behind. That night, Lewis broke out "a Skant proportion" of the portable soup.

On September 19, after six miles, Lewis and his party noted that, in the distance, the ridge terminated and there was a large tract of prairie lying to the southwest. They were coming to the end of the Bitterroots. This realization greatly revived the party, despite their weak condition because of weight loss and inadequate food.

Captain Lewis realized that this prairie still was about sixty miles away, but he wanted to reach it as soon as possible. So, on September 22, he ordered a "forced march" to the open country. At 2½ miles, the party encountered Reubin Field, who was bringing them dried fish and roots that Clark had obtained from the Nez Perce. After voraciously downing this welcome food, the group proceeded to a village of friendly Nez Perce Indians, reaching it at 5 o'clock that evening. They had passed over the Bitterroots safely.

Table 6.1 (column 4, October 1805) provides an assessment of their dietary adequacy after this harrowing period. As one might expect, the party's dietary status had reached an all-time low; their intake had been inadequate for all of the nutrients, plus fiber. It is not surprising that the men had been experiencing many health problems recently.

It turned out that most of the men (i.e., Clark and his party, as well as Lewis and his men), became sick after eating the dried fish and roots which had been obtained from the Nez Perce at Weippe Prairie. Most of the men became violently ill for a week or more with acute diarrhea and vomiting, particularly Lewis. It is known that the roots being consumed were camas roots, a staple of the Indians west of the mountains. The cause of this malady has been studied by several students of the Lewis and Clark Expedition. DeVoto attributed it to a sharp change in diet, plus weakness and fatigue.[16] Chuinard also believed that it was due to the drastic change in diet from all meat to all roots and dried fish, but that bacteria on the salmon may also have been a factor.[17] Actually, all of these factors could have contributed to their illness. However, the author has recently discovered information in the literature that introduces the very likely possibility that the men had been poisoned by toxic alkaloids which occur in the White Camas (Death Camas) but not in the more commonly eaten Blue Camas. Botanists have known for some time that there are two main types of camas plants. Unfortunately, these two types of camas tend to share the same habitat, often growing side by side (Figure 6.1). Also, the bulbs and leaves of the White Camas resemble those of the Blue Camas. However, according to Nancy J. Turner, the bulbs and leaves of the former give a burning sensation when touched to the tongue.[18] She cautions that great care must be taken when digging Blue Camas bulbs not to confuse them with White Camas (Figure 6.2). The latter, of course, is most easily distinguished from the Blue Camas while both are still blooming. Turner notes that the aboriginal people within the range of the White Camas were well aware of its poisonous qualities.[19] Within its area of distribution, Death Camas is responsible for the greatest loss of sheep of any poisonous plant.[20] She recommends that anyone wishing to sample Blue Camas bulbs should dig them up at flowering time to avoid any possibility of misidentification.[21] Historically, Camas bulbs have been a staple article of diet for many indigenous groups of the northwestern United States and in British Columbia.[22]

On October 7, when the expedition started down the Clearwater River, Lewis was still recuperating from his two-week bout with dysentery. On October 10, where the Clearwater flows into the Snake River, the corps bought fish from the local Indians and their first dogs. The latter were most welcome since the men had grown very tired of living on fish, at this point. Except for Clark, most of the men liked dog meat, which was fortunate because it was going to be one of their dietary staples for some time now.

As the entourage swept on toward the junction of the Snake with the Columbia, they began to encounter Indians who traveled by canoe. These Indians had more horses than any tribe on the continent; they also had many dogs. But these Indians never ate horse meat and rarely ate dogs. Instead, their diet was primarily deer and elk, supplemented by large quantities of salmon and wapato roots.

The party reached the Columbia on October 16. Not wishing to waste time sending out hunters while going down the river, the captains purchased forty dogs on October 18, just before they set out. During the rest of October, the men lived on dogs, dried fish, and pounded wapato roots, bought from the Indians along the way.

The expedition passed the mouth of Sandy River on November 2. The next night, the party camped on an island across from the mouth of the Williamette River, which became its temporary base of operations.

By now, the men were consuming a great many wapato roots, which agreed with them well. By November 4, Clark was describing them in his field notes as "roundish roots near the Size of a hen's egg roasted," and in his journal entry the same day, he noted that they had "an agreeable taste and answers verry well in place of bread." These roots, along with fish, turned out to be staples for the corps for the rest of their stay on the coast. On November 17, the party moved its camp to a site beyond Point Ellice. Here, game was available, enabling the men to augment their diet with meat. This was their westernmost campsite.

The next important decision was whether the group should winter on the north side or the south side of the river's estuary. There were several issues involved. Obviously, they needed good water, plenty of game, and some shelter. Lewis believed that the south side would be a better location for processing salt, which most of the men craved. And the area abounded in elk, which the men preferred to the deer which were the most common game on the north side. Elk were fatter and much larger. Thus, the party obtained more food for the amount of effort expended. This is another example of the Optimal Foraging Theory in practice.

They took a vote, which ended up in favor of the party's moving to the south side of the river. There, the captains soon found a site which satisfied all of their requirements, including a spring that would provide them with pure, potable water. On December 7, Lewis guided the expedition to the site they named Fort Clatsop. Next day, Clark selected a suitable place to set up the salt-making plant. While some of the men hunted, others started to cut down trees to make huts and a palisade.

The persistent rain in that region not only interfered with building their quarters, it made it impossible to preserve their food. Many of the men were sick or suffering from previous injuries, but the work went forward. Although the huts still lacked roofs, all of the men had moved in by Christmas Eve. By December 30, the fort was completed.

Christmas Day was wet and disagreeable, and Clark noted that there was "nothing to raise our spirits" since their liquor had run out July 4. He wrote, "Our diner concisted of pore Elk, So much Spoiled that we eate it thro' mear necessity, Some Spoiled pounded fish and a fiew roots."

At Fort Clatsop, the men's health problems continued. Many of the problems of the previous summer simply had not gone away. The strenuous portaging and the onerous treks over the Divide and the Bitterroots had been debilitating, leaving them with lessened resistance. Their colds and fevers, as well as the influenza-like condition from which so many of them suffered, undoubtedly were exacerbated by the cold, wet weather and their confined quarters (see Chapter 7). One is reminded of the old saying that an army on the move is much less likely to succumb to contagious disease than one which is stationary.

Venereal disease (particularly syphilis and gonorrhea) was a chronic problem throughout the trip. However, there are relatively few entries in the journals regarding it. Because it was such a common occurrence within the military during this era, the captains might have viewed this health problem (like the undoubtedly recurring bouts of malaria) as unworthy of repeated mention. However, Captain Clark seemed to take this problem more seriously than Captain Lewis. Lewis had extolled the excellent condition of the men in his glowing letter to President Jefferson the day of the corps's departure from Fort Mandan April 7. Yet, only a few days before (March 31, 1805), Clark had expressed a degree of concern regarding this health problem.

Table 6.1 (column 5, March 1806) provides an assessment of the party's dietary adequacy while preparing to depart from Fort Clatsop. Their nutrient intakes had been very similar to those when they left Fort Mandan in April 1805 in that they had had adequate amounts of water, carbohydrate, fat, and total calories, and more than enough protein. They had been obtaining carbohydrates from wapato and other roots, and protein and fat from fish and game. From these same foods, they had obtained borderline-to-adequate amounts of vitamins and minerals, except for folic acid and vitamins C and E. They had not lacked for vitamin A, having obtained carotene from various roots. Their high salmon consumption should have provided precursors of vitamin D, plus iodine. But they had suffered from lack of sunlight. They had a safer water supply than at any time previously. Fiber intake remained fairly low, resulting in constipation and related problems.

What the men really needed now was an over-all balanced diet, less stress, more rest, and time to recover from their physical injuries. But there was no time now for rest and recuperation. The corps wanted to get started for home. The party set out from Fort Clatsop on March 23, 1806, thirty-three people in five canoes. Now, there was much less space for food and supplies, and far fewer bartering items.

On March 31, going up the Columbia, the party stopped at Sauvie Island. Here they remained until April 6, hunting and drying a good supply of meat and bartering for wapato roots from the natives. This supply of food would probably have to last them now until they arrived at the Nez Perce lodges.

Having decided to go overland beyond the Dalles, and having obtained sufficient horses from the Indians to do so, they began to go almost due east across the arid plains of southeastern Washington. Clark wrote that, on May 3, they consumed the last of the dried meat and the balance of their dogs. This meal "made a scant supper," he said, "and not anything for tomorrow." On May 4, they set out early, and halted at the lodge of six families. Here, they purchased two lean dogs and a few large cakes of half-cured bread made out of a root (probably "cows" or biscuit-root). Lewis described biscuit-root as resembling the sweet potato: "with these we made some soope, and took breakfast."

When they arrived at Twisted Hair's village, it became apparent that food was very scarce among all of the Nez Perce at this time. However, one of the Indian leaders told Clark that, in view of the excellent medical care Clark had given them the year before, his people would like to trade food in return for more medical care. The captains agreed to this arrangement, and for the next six weeks Captain Clark cared for the sick.

On May 7, the Indians told the party that because of the heavy snows the snow melt was delayed. Therefore, no passage would be possible until about the first of June. This was bad news for the men, who were constantly hungry. Fortunately, they began to obtain deer and other game by May 8. And, in return for medical care, the Nez Perce were giving the party camas, bread of cows, and an occasional colt or dried fish. But still it was not enough. The men were forced to go out hunting every day now, each one responsible for his own food. Meanwhile, Clark treated the Indians for many ailments, including eye problems, a woman with an abscess, a little girl with rheumatism, scrofula (tuberculosis of the lymph glands), ulcers, loss of the use of limbs, and paralysis. Eye problems were the most common complaints, for which Clark gave them soothing "eye water." These eye problems were probably caused by such vitamin deficiencies as riboflavin, vitamin C, vitamin A, trachoma (a virus), or gonorrhea, a common condition among the Indians. During this time, Clark also treated members of his own party: the teething problems and mumps of Sacagawea's toddler and Private Bratton's bad back coupled with general muscle weakness from his enforced inactivity.

On June 15, the party started out to go over the Bitterroots by themselves since the guides had insisted it was still too soon to go. However, they were forced to retreat due to snow as deep as twelve-to-fifteen-feet. On June 18 the captains decided to send Drouillard and Shannon to the Nez Perce lodges to obtain a guide. They finally returned on June 23rd, surprisingly with three guides. And early on the morning of June 24th they started back toward the Bitterroots again.

Continuing their climb with the help of the experienced guides, they camped on the side of Spring Mountain at 6,500 feet on June 27. Clark had been fighting a splitting headache for two days, possibly from altitude changes, and the men had exhausted their meat supply. So the captains distributed a pint of bear oil to be placed in each of their four mess kettles, mixing it with boiled roots. According to Clark, it was "an agreeable dish."

Three days later the hunters managed to kill six deer, which would provide the men with a plentiful supper. The party arrived at Travelers' Rest just before sunset, the guides having saved the expedition.

On the morning of July 3, the captains and their respective parties said goodbye and separated. Clark planned to go to Three Forks and then down the Yellowstone River. Meanwhile, Lewis and nine men, with five Nez Perce guides and seventeen horses, set out northward down the Bitterroot River. Next day, July 4, their Nez Perce guides left them to go home, and Lewis's party proceeded northeast on their own. When they got to Great Falls, they followed the Missouri to the mouth of the Marias. Throughout this leg of their trip, there had been ample amounts of deer, followed later by an abundance of buffalo, elk, and bear.

On July 16, as Lewis and his party of three men began to follow the Marias River upstream, they passed immense herds of buffalo. Buffalo meat proved to be the major source of subsistence for these men during the Marias venture. In fact, during their forced march back to the mouth of the Marias on July 28 while fleeing from the Piegan Indians, they were fortunate enough to kill a buffalo during one of their infrequent stops. They dressed and consumed this animal on the spot.

Captain Lewis's small party managed to get to the Missouri just in time to meet Ordway and his men coming down the Missouri from the Falls. The Marias venture had taken about thirteen days. Because this was a relatively short period, it is not surprising that Lewis and his party did not seem to have suffered from having consumed virtually nothing but buffalo meat during this time.

The worst accident of the expedition occurred as Lewis and his party proceeded downstream to meet the Clark party. On August 11, the men had spied some elk on the northeast shore. They put in, and Lewis and Private Pierre Cruzatte set out to replenish their meat supply. Lewis had killed one and Cruzatte had wounded another. Then, suddenly, Lewis was hit by a bullet in his left thigh, an inch below his hip joint. It then came out on the right side, leaving a three-inch gash the width of the ball.

It turned out that Cruzatte, who was blind in one eye and nearsighted in the other, had shot Lewis by mistake. Lewis hobbled back to the canoes, and Sergeant Gass helped him take off his clothes. Later, Lewis wrote, "I...dressed my wounds myself as well as I could introducing tents of patent lint [rolls of cotton] into the ball holes...." This was done so the wound would stay open and new tissue could grow from the inside out.[23] Lewis added, "The wounds blead considerably but I was hapy to find that [the bullet] had touched neither bone nor artery." Here Lewis demonstrated his medical savvy. That night, he developed a high fever for which he self-administered a poultice of Peruvian bark. On the morning of August 12, he was still stiff and sore, but the fever had receded—probably thanks to the Peruvian bark, the captains' standard remedy for fevers. Nevertheless, the pain persisted.

That afternoon, Lewis and his men overtook Captain Clark and his men near the mouth of the Yellowstone. It was August 12, just as they had planned. On the 13th, the reunited party embarked for the Mandan villages, where they enjoyed a three-day visit with their Indian friends.

By August 17, the men had resumed their homeward trip down the Missouri. At first, buffalo, elk, and deer, as well as plums, were plentiful. This food was especially welcome since their own food supplies now were gone. By September, the party began to encounter traders. The men welcomed them, not only for the news they brought, but also for the tobacco, whiskey, and other provisions they offered. On September 14, they met traders sent out by the Chouteaus of St. Louis who gave them whiskey, biscuit, pork, and onions. Undoubtedly, these men were most pleased to eat "biscuit" again, having been deprived for so long of this southern favorite.

By September 18, the party was nearing the settlements; they had run completely out of provisions and trade foods. This scarcity of food was due in part to the increased passage of traders' boats which had caused the deer and bear to move back from the river. Because this meant disembarking and hunting far afield, the men decided instead to subsist on "poppaws" (plums), which were readily available near shore. Meanwhile, both Shannon and Potts were complaining of sore eyes because of prolonged exposure to the sun.

Table 6.1 (column 6, September 1806) provides an assessment of the corps's dietary adequacy as they were about to complete their journey. Since the men had proceeded along rivers almost the entire time since leaving Fort Clatsop, they had had ready access to water, though it may not always have been safe. Nevertheless, fluid intake should have been adequate. Total calorie intake had been reasonably sufficient because of the ready availability of game, except for the last few days of the trip. Most of the time, the consumption of protein and fat had ranged from adequate to more than adequate. Except for getting "biscuit" from the traders, there seems to have been essentially no intake of bread products nor consumption of sweets or vegetables. So intake of fiber and carbohydrate was low and borderline, respectively. Certain vitamins and minerals associated with cereal products, vegetables, and fruits were low. Intakes of vitamins A, C, D, folic acid, and riboflavin were low, as was iodine. No mention was made of milk consumption or of eating other calcium-containing foods, so calcium intake must have been low.

By today's standards, the diets of the men during the expedition were not ideal. Overall, they had a very low fiber intake, occasionally, too much fat, and frequently, too much protein. They had many nutrient deficiencies which would have resulted in manifold symptoms as well as a seriously decreased ability to function, had the expedition continued much longer.

Intakes of folic acid, vitamin C, vitamin E, and calcium were continuously low, and riboflavin, vitamin A (carotene), magnesium, and iodine were borderline to low most of the time. Considering the party's constant exposure to the sun without the ultraviolet ray protection of today's sunglasses, coupled with the lack of both vitamin C and riboflavin, it is not surprising that they suffered from chronic eye problems. They also were suffering from boils, other skin conditions, and slow wound healing. In addition, they complained of a wide range of aches and pains. All of these conditions are typical early symptoms of scurvy, caused by vitamin C deficiency.

Overt symptoms reflecting some of these dietary lacks would not develop until later. For example, osteoporosis would not appear until middle age or beyond. A continued low intake of iodine would have eventually resulted in goiter for many of the men. The youthfulness of the men and the relative brevity of the trip were critical factors in the corps's ability to withstand the variety of stresses, dietary deficiencies, and other health problems experienced, as well as it did.

Chapter 7
Food, Nutrition, and Health Aspects of the Expedition

Throughout the expedition, there were variations in the food supply. The party was particularly sensitive to the amounts of small and large game available, since, overall, wild game constituted its main source of food. The men had hunted small game while wintering at Camp Dubois, and they continued to obtain quantities of deer and elk after leaving St. Louis as they went up the lower Missouri during the summer of 1804. Then, on August 23, the men killed their first buffalo beyond the mouth of the Big Sioux River in South Dakota. Soon after, in mid-September, they began to see goats and great quantities of buffalo near the confluence of the White River with the Missouri. Many of these animals were migrating back to the Black Hills for the winter after a summer of succulent grazing on the plains. And they soon became primary sources for food for the corps. Later in the fall, some of the buffalo that remained on the plains became a staple food while the party wintered with the Mandan Indians during the winter of 1804-1805. They continued to see immense herds of buffalo after leaving Fort Mandan in April 1805. Indeed, the hunting was unsurpassed for about two months, with the men obtaining not only buffalo, but elk, antelope, and deer as well. Above the mouth of the Musselshell River, where they moved into a drier ecosystem with less grass, they saw less of the buffalo. From Great Falls to Three Forks, it became necessary for the men to rely on smaller animals. However, game still was abundant.

Food became scarce for the corps after they arrived at the Continental Divide, and the situation became much worse as they crossed the Bitterroots, where there was little to hunt but grouse. The party survived, mainly because of the relatively short duration of the trip (September 3-22, 1805), the use of their emergency rations of portable soup, and the sacrifice of three colts en route.

Vicissitudes in the availability of game continued as the corps made its way to the Pacific Ocean and wintered at Fort Clatsop, as well as during its journey back to St. Louis, where they arrived in September 1806.

Historically, the location and availability of game has never been static. They are the net result of interactions among a number of factors at any given time, and these factors may change more dramatically during certain times or eras than others. The situations regarding game availability which Lewis and Clark encountered on their journey were the net result of many previous conditions and events, which had contributed to the changing availabilities of game that occurred.

After leaving St. Louis, as the Lewis and Clark party went up the Missouri, they began to view a grassland area which had been home to teeming numbers of megafauna from the time of the end of the Pleistocene Era. But, by about 10,000 B.C., the Paleo-Indian inhabitants of these plains had learned to make tools, such as massive spearheads and missile weapons. These tools enabled them to obtain greater quantities of meat than the crude foraging techniques that they had used previously. Large herd animals became dietary staples, including forms of bison and mammoth which are now extinct. Their extinction probably was caused by the change in climate, which became hotter and drier because of the glacial retreat. These conditions led to less bountiful grasslands upon which the megafauna subsisted. The scarcity of grass then led to a sharp reduction in the numbers of large animals, which in turn led to overkilling by human predators. It is widely believed that these two circumstances together led to the extinction of two-thirds of the large mammals once native to western North America.

What Lewis and Clark were seeing in 1804 was a later form of bison, which turned out to be a (seasonal) dietary staple for the Plains Indians of the early nineteenth century, who, by then, were occupying these grasslands. Not only had these animals survived, but in some areas of North America they had become quite numerous. The journals of Lewis and Clark provide on-going reports of game availability. At Fort Mandan, the party participated in buffalo hunts with the Mandan Indians, sometimes with unbelievable success. Upon leaving Fort Mandan in early April 1805, the men initially encountered very little game, probably because of heavy local hunting by the Hidatsa and Assiniboine Indians. But by late April, as they moved toward the mouth of the Yellowstone, both captains reported seeing immense quantities of bison, as well as elk and pronghorns. At Great Falls, Lewis reported an estimated 10,000 bison at one sighting.

Paul Martin and Christine Szuter propose two possible explanations for the abundance of bison despite the presence of skilled hunters. The first is that it was caused by the sharp reduction in the Indian population following European contact, in large part due to pandemic diseases which repeatedly erupted, destroying 50-95% of the native population.[1] A second explanation for such large numbers of game animals is that there existed a war zone, or buffer phenomenon, a consequence of intertribal warfare or tensions. Within an intertribal buffer zone, or no-man's land, high-ranked prey found shelter, a situation which favored great population increases in game animals. Martin and Szuter suggest that this abundance of game along the Missouri was reflective of an area which served as a buffer zone, depopulated by warfare, disease, or both. War parties of various tribes were ever at hand, and anyone hunting, processing or drying meat, or trapping was at risk of being killed. As a prime example of this fate, these authors point to George Drouillard and John Potts, former members of the Lewis and Clark party who were both killed when they returned a few years later to trap at Three Forks. The authors estimate that this Upper Missouri War Zone extended west from the mouth of the Yellowstone up both rivers to Three Forks[2] (Figure 5.2). Captain Clark himself seems to have recognized this phenomenon. On August 29, 1806, he wrote, "I have observed that in the country between the nations which are at war with each other the greatest numbers of wild animals are to be found."

Once the corps proceeded upstream from Great Falls, the buffalo disappeared and other big game became scarce. Traversing the Bitterroots in September 1805 the corps encountered virtually no game. By early fall, this region's customary lack of game had become exacerbated by the heavy snow and cold which the party encountered as they ascended in altitude.

West of the Rockies, Lewis and Clark noted another major drop in large game animals, which they found difficult to understand considering the rich loess soils they were observing, plus the fact that, from information they gleaned from various sources, the Indian population in the Columbia drainage area totaled only about 80,000 people at that time.[3] Moreover, this land supported huge numbers of free-roving horses, "many as fat as seals," according to Lewis's journal entry of April 25, 1806. The question undoubtedly arises, if this intermontane area were so ideal for horses, why were there no bison or elk and so few pronghorn or deer there?

The most likely answer is that the Columbia basin was, in actuality, potentially good for both horses and for wild game. The Indians of the extended Nez Perce nation owned more horses than any other group on the continent, but they almost never hunted them for food. Instead, these Indians were exploiting wild game of the types cited above. Although they were reasonably well supported by fish and roots, they also were fond of hunting wild megafauna at every opportunity, sharply reducing their numbers. It is fortuitous that, in spite of this hunting behavior on the part of local Indians, Lewis and Clark's party was able to survive largely on elk in the heavily forested (thus protected) area around Fort Clatsop during the winter of 1806.

An interesting example of the changing status of game availability is that which has occurred over the past 200 years in the Bitterroot Mountains. During the expedition of Lewis and Clark game was scarce in the Bitterroots. The men frequently noted that there was nothing to eat there but grouse. In 1805, the choice game animals were down on the plains during the summer, enjoying the grass of the War Zone described earlier. Then, in the fall, they migrated as far as the Black Hills or the shrub-steppe of the Rockies for the winter. But with the opening up of the Louisiana Territory, as farmers and ranchers began moving onto the plains the game was driven back into the mountains. Today, the Bitterroots are considered prime big-game country. According to Stephen Ambrose, "...out of state hunters [now] pay hundreds of dollars for a license and an outfitter to hunt elk and bear in these mountains."[4]

The question frequently arises as to why the Lewis and Clark party (and sometimes the various Indian tribes) failed to make more use of fish. The Snake Indians complained bitterly to Lewis about their inability to possess guns like the Plains Indians.[5] Without guns, they said, they were at the mercy of these Indians, forced to hide in the mountains most of the year, nearly starving to death. One wonders why they did not make better use of the fish that were in the adjacent rivers. The Lewis and Clark party often fished erratically even when fish were available. Beginning July 22, 1804, the men caught catfish while coming up the Missouri. An exceptionally large catch of mixed fish was obtained by dragging Maha Creek on August 16, 1804. The next mention of fishing did not occur until June 11, 1805, when Goodrich caught some trout in the Great Falls area. Later, on August 19, before going over the Divide in a desperate attempt to augment the food supply, Lewis had a seine put out. It yielded 528 fish, most of which he distributed to the Indians who had come over to meet the corps. Then, going down the Columbia, and at Fort Clatsop, the party tended to buy dried salmon from the natives rather than fishing for those which were then in season.

On the other hand, the Indians of the Columbia drainage area seemed to have fully exploited the fishing resource, catching immense amounts of salmon when they were in season and preserving them. The journals note that Killamuck Indians gathered sturgeon and other fish thrown up by the waves and left by the tide when salmon were out of season. Both the Lewis and Clark party and the Indians seemed reluctant to utilize foods other than their accustomed dietary staples (e.g., large and small game). This behavior supports the long-held belief of nutritionists that people tend to prefer food to which they are accustomed. Unfortunately, this preference often exacerbates situations involving food scarcity.

Anthropologists believe that people instinctively adhere to Yesner's Optimal Foraging Theory, preferring those food resources which provide the greatest nutrient density for the least expenditure of effort.[6] This attitude also can magnify the problems attendant with food scarcity.

The extent of Sacagawea's contribution to the party's food supply has grown as she has assumed the mythical persona described by anthropologists as "woman the gatherer."[7] One gets the impression that, by assiduously digging roots for the corps, she single-handedly kept the men fed from the time they left Fort Mandan in April 1805 until the party returned there in August 1806. At the very least, this view is unrealistic. Even if sufficient roots had been available, it would have been a Herculean task to be accomplished daily by one woman. Further, even a large amount of roots collected daily would not meet the men's nutritional and energy needs. Vegetable foods are indeed important nutritionally, but they simply do not compare with meat in nutrient density and calorie content. The activity levels of these men were very high, demanding a high caloric intake, at times at least twice that of an active farmer. In such a situation, meat, with its fat and protein content, was by far a more realistic staple.

Sacagawea has been criticized for not digging bitterroots for the men when they were beset with food scarcity while going over the Bitterroot Mountains in the fall of 1805. Digging for bitterroots would not have solved the problem. Not only did the men not like the bitterroots, snowfall accumulations meant that roots would have been hard to find. Further, to bring the needed amount of roots back to camp and process them for thirty-three people would have presented a difficult logistical problem. Finally, Sacagawea also had an infant to care for.

An objective evaluation of Sacagawea's contribution to the party's food supply would recognize that she did dig roots for the men, but only occasionally. There are three instances when she dug roots for the party soon after leaving Fort Mandan, when the corps was still in an ecosystem familiar to her. She dug the Jerusalem artichoke, the wild licorice, and the white apple (or breadroot). Before leaving the Nez Perce to go back over the Bitterroots in 1806, she dried some fennel for use during the trip. Though this herb is useful as a flavoring agent, it does not serve as a source of food. During the time that the party was at Fort Clatsop, the journals do not indicate that either Sacagawea or any of the men went out to dig roots. In summary, Sacagawea's sporadic offerings lent much-needed variety and flavor to the party's otherwise monotonous diet. They did not, however, provide substantial nutritional support or fend off starvation. Unquestionably, her most valuable contributions to the expedition were her services as diplomat, interpreter, and guide. Her services as a guide were confined, understandably, to times when the party was in the areas that were familiar to her from her childhood—at Three Forks; going across the Divide; and, later, in the summer of 1806, accompanying Clark's sub-group exploring the Yellowstone Valley. Moulton has said it well: "Sacagawea has attracted much attention in this century from historians and writers of fiction, but the amount written about her far exceeds the actual information about her life and personality."[8] Unfortunately, misinformation regarding Sacagawea serves to obfuscate the limited reliable information that exists about her.

Another question frequently posed concerns the site chosen for processing salt from seawater while wintering at Fort Clatsop. Individuals sometimes ask why the captains chose a site so far away from camp and/or the mouth of the Columbia? First, the camp was on the Netul River.[9] They wanted seawater, not the muddy water of a small river. The tidewater area was not suitable either. It tended to be very rough and stormy in this estuary area. Moreover, the water there was a mixture of Columbia River water and seawater from the ocean. In choosing water from which to process salt, Lewis and Clark knew that the higher the salt content, the better. They found what seemed to be an ideal place close to the coast, fifteen miles south and east of the fort. Here, at today's Seaside, Oregon, they could process pure ocean water. The men at the salt works managed to obtain twenty gallons of processed salt for the party's use going back.[10]

From the time they crossed the Divide until they reached the Pacific, the party had encountered four main root staples: the bitterroot, camas or camassia, cous or breadroot, and wapato root. Although bitterroot was a staple of the Indians who lived in the Bitterroot Mountain ecosystem, it proved to be unpopular with the men. Camas made them sick on the way west, but, going back, it seemed to agree with them. As discussed in Chapter 6, it seems likely that, on the way to the Pacific, either by accident or design,* the men had been given some camas roots which contained the deadly white camas. Going back, the men obviously were eating roots from the blue camas (apparently the more plentiful species of camas plants). Since the roots themselves have an identical appearance, it is possible that some white camas bulbs had been included inadvertently. Unfortunately, none of us who are alive today were there at the time. Thus, there is no way of obtaining a final answer to this tantalizing question. One can only conjecture, based on whatever information is available. Harry Thompson has pointed out that this situation represents a never-ending problem for historians as they attempt to reconstruct the past and determine conclusively what took place.[12]

Both the cous (breadroot) and wapato, staples of the Nez Perces and other Indians in the Columbia River drainage, were well-received and well-tolerated by the corps. From a dietary point of view, roots contain mainly digestible complex carbohydrates, fiber, and water. In addition, they usually contain some sugar and the vitamins and minerals generally associated with root vegetables:[13] carotenes, some vitamin C, and potassium. However, roots are low in total calories and in many of the vitamins and minerals contained in meat, such as iron, sodium, and the B-vitamins.

Dried salmon was readily available for purchase by the party. However, while wintering at Fort Clatsop, the men, whenever possible, chose to hunt game instead, which served as their chief protein source. Elk was the most commonly eaten game, along with deer. In December 1805 they had the rare opportunity of eating whale meat. However, this represented an exotic taste experience rather than a regular dietary item.

A frequently asked question is, which meats provide the most protein? The muscle meat from various mammals, and vertebrates in general, is strikingly similar in protein content. As vertebrates evolved, widely different species developed muscles which were very similar biochemically. Meat averages seven grams of protein per ounce. Fat meat will contain somewhat less, and lean meat somewhat more, of protein and water respectively. Some people believe that it is critical to their well-being to choose meat that will provide the most protein per ounce. This concern is unwarranted, because if one is eating as much meat as most Americans today, and, certainly, as much as the corps was consuming, one is

---

*Charles Saunders referred to "a crafty practice of the Klamath medicine men, who would sometimes make a mixture of tobacco, dried iris root, and Death Camas, and give it to a person in order to nauseate him. Then they would charge the victim a fee to make him well again!"[11]

already eating much more protein than is needed or even wise. Such a surfeit of protein places an unnecessary strain on the organs of digestion and excretion.

On July 13, 1805, on the upper Missouri, Lewis noted that it required four deer, or an elk and a deer, or one buffalo daily to supply the men "plentifully." This would be equal to about 4½ pounds of meat per person. In fact, during the eighty-day period spanning April 25-July 13, 1805, until their arrival at Great Falls, the men had been consuming nine pounds of meat daily.[14] Such intakes of meat are clearly unhealthful.[15] The party was eating that much meat because meat essentially constituted their sole source of food during this period and also the main source of calories and protein. In contrast, those of us today who consume a balanced diet of fruits, vegetables, whole-grain products, dairy products, and meat get most of our calories from carbohydrate and fat and a lesser amount from protein. Recommended intakes are as follows: carbohydrate (50-55%), fat (25-30%), and protein, (10-20%).

The continued sickness of the men at Fort Clatsop is puzzling. After all, they had experienced much more demanding situations previously, such as pulling the boats up the muddy lower Missouri, portaging, and making their way over the Bitterroots. And once the fort was built, they stayed in the same place for about three months. Their main activities consisted of going out to hunt and/or interacting with the local Indians. Yet they were suffering continuously from respiratory diseases and other illnesses, and many of their physical problems caused by previous injuries incurred during the expedition stubbornly refused to disappear.

The damp, dreary weather undoubtedly contributed to their health problems. But a more compelling factor may have been the party's crowded living quarters. Except for the winter at Fort Mandan, the men had slept mainly outdoors in the open air, on the ground, or in tents. At Fort Clatsop, however, the men were living under much more confined conditions. Fort Clatsop was about fifty feet square, and consisted of two long, facing structures joined on the sides by palisaded walls. Between the buildings was a parade ground about fifty feet by twenty feet. This left thirty feet for the width of the two structures, each about fifteen feet deep. One structure contained four rooms: one for the captains; one for Charbonneau, Sacagawea, and their young toddler, Jean Baptiste; one room served as an orderly room; and the fourth, the smoke house.[16] The other structure, also fifty by fifteen feet, was divided into three rooms for the enlisted men. Allowing for outside walls and partitions between the rooms, each room probably was about fifteen by sixteen feet. Adding to the crowded condition was the low ceiling of the rooms, which prevented the men from walking upright in them.[17] With about ten men per room (plus their clothing and other belongings), and no good ventilating system, it was inevitable that contagious diseases would be passed continuously from one person to another.

Throughout the expedition, the captains had been treating the men for venereal diseases which they were contracting from the Indian women they encountered along the way. However, this health problem was greatly under-reported in the journals, probably because it was such a common occurrence among military men during this era. The problem had been anticipated, judging by the medicines and medical equipment that had been purchased for the trip. The men continued to have sex at Fort Clatsop, but they paid the price for this activity by contracting venereal disease. Captain Lewis treated the affected men with mercurous chloride ointment, as he had with George Gibson at Fort Mandan.[18] However, the apparent cure was only temporary. Six months later, Silas

Goodrich and Hugh McNeal were exhibiting symptoms of the secondary stage of syphilis.[19] By 1828, Clark had listed them both as dead, possibly as a result of the disease.[20]

Another frequently asked question is whether Captain Lewis had a mental illness. One can learn much about Lewis from the frequency with which he made journal entries and from his style of writing, which often varied considerably from one time to another. His pattern of making entries in his journal was erratic. There were long periods when there were no entries at all, even though important things were happening. Clark, on the other hand, stolidly wrote in his journal almost daily throughout the trip.

Captain Lewis made his first journal entry when he began going down the Ohio, August 31, 1803. He was at his best when recording objective information, e.g., the flora and fauna which he encountered along the way. He seems to have made few, if any, entries while the party was at Camp Dubois on the Wood River. However, his lack of record-keeping probably can be excused because he was in St. Louis most of this time, carrying out diplomatic, political, and business duties for the party. Clark faithfully made entries, but because he often failed to include detail much potentially important information regarding this period is missing. Clark may have felt that, since the expedition had not yet formally begun, it was unnecessary to make detailed entries. One omission that has been especially criticized is his failure to make regular entries regarding the health of his men while at Camp Dubois.[21] However, he frequently noted his own health problems.

Once the expedition formally began, there were long periods ranging from months to nearly a year during which Lewis's entries appear to have been both few and sporadic: i.e., May 14, 1804, to April 7, 1805; August 26, 1805, to January 1, 1806; and from August 12 to the end of September, 1806. However, there is still the possibility that the missing entries simply were lost.[22]

Lewis experienced wide mood swings, ranging from periods of mania (or, at the very least, hypomania), to bouts of depression, as noted by Stephen Ambrose, Gerald Snyder, and others.[23] Providing compelling support for this view is President Jefferson, who had observed these traits in Captain Lewis. In his letter of August 18, 1813, to Paul Allen, editor of James Hosmer's two volume *History of the Expedition of Captains Lewis and Clark*, Jefferson wrote:

> Governor Lewis had from early life been subject to hypochondriac affections. It was a constitutional disposition in all the nearer branches of the family of his name, & was more immediately inherited by him from his father. They had not however been so strong as to give uneasiness to his family. While he lived with me in Washington, I observed at times sensible depressions of mind, but knowing their constitutional source, I estimated their course by what I had seen in the family. During his Western expedition the constant exertion which that required of all the faculties of body & mind, suspended these distressing affections; but after his establishment at St. Louis in sedentary occupations they returned upon him with redoubled vigor, and began seriously to alarm his friends....[24]

Lewis's journal entry, as well as his letter to President Jefferson, both written the day the party departed from Mandan (April 7, 1805) and of similar content, are strongly suggestive of a hypomanic state. In his journal entry for that day, Lewis was even more effusive than in his letter. However, he was showing less bravado, actually indicating some qualms about the upcoming leg of the journey:

Our vessels consisted of six small canoes and two large perogues. This little fleet altho' not quite so rispectable as those of Columbus or Capt. Cook, were still viewed by us with as much anxiety for their safety and preservation. we were now about to penetrate a country at least two thousand miles in width, on which the foot of civilized man has never trodden; the good or evil it had in store for us was for experiment yet to determine, and these little vessells contained every article by which we were to expect to subsist or defend ourselves. however, as the state of mind in which we are, generally gives the colouring to events, when the imagination is suffered to wander into futurity, the picture which now presented itself to me was a most pleasing one, enterta[in]ing as I do, the most confident hope of succeeding in a voyage which formed a da[r]ling project of mine for the last ten years, I could but esteem this moment of my departure as among the most happy of my life. The party are in excellent health and sperits, zealously attached to the enterprise, and anxious to proceed; not a whisper of murmur or discontent to be heard among them, but all act in unison, and with the most perfict harmoney.[25]

In contrast to Lewis's letter and journal entry, Clark's last journal entry prior to departure from Mandan, dated March 31, 1805, showed guarded concern about the men. He wrote, "All the party in high Sperits....Generally helthy except Venerials Complaints which is verry Common amongst the natives and the men Catch it from them."[26] This is one of the relatively few entries in the journals which specifically mention the problem of venereal disease among the party members.

Another of Lewis's journal entries that suggests that he had manic tendencies is one dated June 11, 1806. Here, he provided a long and verbose description (about 1,500 words) of the camas plant and the elaborate procedures followed by the Chopunnish (Nez Perce) Indians in preparing it for their consumption as a staple food.[27] Fortunately, and perhaps even inadvertently, this detailed process may have removed the poisonous alkaloids of the white camas, should it have been present in a given batch of camus roots. Moreover, Lewis had a bout with malaria while going down the Ohio in November 1804. It is highly probable that he suffered later from recurrences of this disease,[28] which could have exacerbated any innate emotional instability that he may have possessed.

Of the thirty-three people who left Fort Mandan to go to the Pacific and back, comprising the "permanent party," twenty-nine people completed the journey to St. Louis. John Colter had left the party on August 17, 1806, just before the corps left Mandan for St. Louis, to join two fur trappers, Joseph Dickson and Forrest Hancock, in their Yellowstone venture. So, as the corps went downstream, Colter went back upstream and back to the wilderness. After exploring the West with his two companions for a time, Colter joined the St. Louis Missouri Fur Company. In 1807-08, while traveling alone in search of Indians with whom to trade, he became the first known white American to penetrate the country that today comprises Yellowstone National Park.[29]

Table 7.1 summarizes the known vital statistics for the members of the permanent party who left Fort Mandan together on April 7, 1805. It gives the dates of birth and death of these individuals, insofar as they can be determined, and the cause of death if known. The average age at enlistment of those for whom birth dates are known was twenty-eight, with a range from age sixteen (George Shannon) to thirty-four years (John Shields). Neither the birth nor death dates are known for eight members of the permanent party: Pierre Cruzatte, Silas Goodrich, Francois Labiche, Jean Baptiste Lepage, Hugh McNeal,

Table 7.1 Vital Statistics of the Lewis and Clark Permanent Party[a]

Name	Birth and Death	Age at Death	Cause of Death
Lewis, Meriwether	1774-1809	35	Suicide
Clark, William	1770-1838	68	Unkown
York[b]	ca. 1770-1820+	50+	Cholera
Drouillard, George	? -1810	early 40s?	Killed by Blackfeet
Charbonneau, Toussaint[c]	ca. 1758-1834/38	81-85	Old age?
Sacagawea[d]	ca. 1788-1812	24	Fever[e]
Charbonneau, Baptiste[f]	1805-1866	61	Pneumonia
Enlisted Men			
Bratton, William	1778-1841	63	Unknown
Collins, John[g]	1775*-1823	48*	Unknown
Colter, John	ca. 1775-1813	38	Jaundice[h]
Cruzatte, Pierre	dates unknown	—	Killed by Blackfeet
Field, Joseph	ca. 1772-1807	35	Unknown
Field, Reubin	ca. 1771-1823	52	Unknown
Frazer, Robert[g]	1775*-1837	62*	Unknown
Gass, Patrick	1771-1870	99	Old age
Gibson, George[g]	1775*-1809	34*	Unknown
Goodrich, Silas	dates unknown	—	Possibly syphilis
Hall, Hugh	1772-?	—	Unknown
Howard, Thomas	1779-?	—	Unknown
Labiche, Francis	dates unknown	—	Unknown
Lepage, Baptiste	dates unknown	—	Unknown
McNeal, Hugh	dates unknown	—	Possibly syphilis
Ordway, John	1775-ca. 1817	42	Unknown
Potts, John	1776-1808	32	Killed by Blackfeet
Pryor, Nathaniel	1772-1831	59	Unknown
Shannon, George[i]	1787-1836	49	Unknown
Shields, John	1769-1809	40	Unknown
Thompson, John B.	dates unknown	—	Unknown
Weiser, Peter	1781- ?	—	Unknown
Werner, William	dates unknown	—	Unknown
Whitehouse, Joseph[j]	ca. 1775-1860	ca. 85	Old age
Willard, Alexander	1778-1865	87	Old age
Windsor, Richard	dates unknown	—	Unknown

a. Unless indicated otherwise, data below were obtained from Moulton, 1986(2).
b. York was considered to be about the same age as Clark (born 1770); date of death estimated from Snyder, 1970:199, and Duncan and Burns, 1997:213.
c. Moulton, 1987(3), 229n: Discharged in 1839, evidently dead by 1843; Thomas and Ronnefeldt, 1982:8.
d. Duncan and Burns 1997:214. Died in 1812 from a fever.
e. Fever probably due to a recurrence of pelvic inflammatory disease. (p. 61)
f. Year of death: Duncan and Burns, 1997:215.
g. Year of birth estimated using mean year of birth of enlisted men for whom birth years are known; asterisks denote estimated year of birth and age at death.
h. Symptomatic of yellow fever, endemic in St. Louis area at that time.
i. Thwaites, 1959(1): xl.
j. Approximate year of death, 1860: Moulton, 1997(11): xvi.

John Thompson, William Werner and Richard Windsor. There are three men whose dates of birth are known but for whom their dates of death are unknown: Privates Hall, Howard, and Weiser. There are three men whose years of death (or approximate dates of death) are known but whose recorded birth dates are unavailable. For these individuals, since the enlistees were fairly close in age, the average year of birth of the fifteen enlisted men whose birth dates are known (i.e., 1775) was used as the estimated date of birth (D.O.B.) for these men. The lifespan of these men (Privates Collins, Frazer, and Gibson) was then estimated using this value and their known year of death. The mean lifespan for these three men was forty-eight years, versus a mean lifespan of about fifty-seven years for the twelve enlisted men for whom there were complete data (Table 7.1). Mean life-span for the combined groups was fifty-five. Age at death ranged from thirty-two (Private John Potts) to ninety-nine (Sergeant Patrick Gass). None of the enlisted men lived beyond sixty-three except Private Whitehouse, Private Willard, and Sergeant Gass, who died at eighty-five, eighty-seven, and ninety-nine, respectively. Clearly, these three men were "outliers." The longevity of Gass is especially noteworthy. He lost an eye during the War of 1812, after which he returned to his home town of Wellsburg, Virginia, and lived in a room-and-board house. On March 31, 1831, at age fifty-nine, Gass married Maria Hamilton, the sixteen-year-old daughter of the man who owned this lodging place. She bore him seven children before dying of measles on February 16, 1847.[30] Despite his long history of heavy whiskey drinking and the ravages of frontier life, Gass's health remained superb. His drinking habits are well documented by Carol L. MacGregor.[31] His accounts show that he bought a large amount of whiskey despite his modest pension of $96 per year, paid annually in two installments of $48. MacGregor states that "The largest part of the purchases noted in Gass's account book does not comprise items necessary for survival...none loom like the composite body of purchases to support his own habits.... Gass bought whiskey, tobacco, coffee and patent medicines....[He] loved coffee and tobacco, but his particular fondness for spirituous drink can now be grounded.... Now it appears on the hard pages of the purchase records."[32] According to John G. Jacob, Gass "was for many years a slave to the debasing habit that degraded and demoralizes so many of the best, most brilliant and most generous of our race. Intemperance was his besetting sin,...."[33]

Willard married in 1807 and had twelve children. The family emigrated to California in 1852, where he died at eighty-seven, and was buried in Sacramento.[34] Whitehouse lived to approximately age eighty-five, presumably dying of old age.[35] Toussaint Charbonneau, the French-Canadian fur trader and interpreter whom Lewis and Clark had brought on at Fort Mandan, lived to be somewhere between eighty-one and eighty-five. He had lived a life on the move, beset with constant danger, with many liaisons with women and indulging in heavy liquor consumption. His life was far from healthful, with an erratic food supply and virtually no health care.[36] The long lives of Gass, Willard, Whitehouse, and Charbonneau, despite frequently unhealthful lifestyles, may have been due to their genetic make-up.

Three former members of the party died as a result of later encounters with the Blackfeet: interpreter George Drouillard (1810), John Potts (1808), and Pierre Cruzatte (in the mid-1820s).[37] John Colter was almost killed at the same time as Potts but he miraculously escaped. He later settled in La Charrette (near St. Louis) and married, dying in 1813 of jaundice[38] (probably yellow fever).

According to Reuben Gold Thwaites, George Shannon, the youngest of the enlisted men, assisted Nicholas Biddle of Philadelphia in the editing of the journals in 1910 (published in 1914). He helped by interpreting the notebooks and in giving personal recollections regarding the expedition. Shannon became a lawyer; he died suddenly in court in 1836 at age 49.[39] Sacagawea died during the winter of 1812 at Fort Manuel in what is now South Dakota. She had given birth to a daughter, Lisette, and later in the winter developed a fever and died.[40] It is probable that she was experiencing another attack of pelvic inflammatory disease (P.I.D.), from which she recovered in June, 1805, but which, this time, proved fatal. After her death, it is believed that Captain Clark assumed responsibility for both of the Charbonneau children.[41] Jean Baptiste Charbonneau died of pneumonia in 1866 at age 61 while following a wagon train en route to Montana in search of gold.[42]

The birth date of Drouillard is not known. Always regarded as a senior member of the party, he probably was at least as old as Clark. Therefore, when he was killed by the Blackfeet in 1810, he probably was in his early forties.

Captain Lewis died in August 1809 presumably by his own hand. Undoubtedly, both personal and professional problems were important factors in leading him to commit this final act. Captain Clark died in 1838, after living a full and successful life. Both of these men received 1,600 acres of land as a reward for their efforts in leading this historic expedition, plus $1,228 in double pay. In addition, President Jefferson rewarded them by naming Lewis Governor of Louisiana Territory in 1807, while Clark was named Brigadier General of Militia of Louisiana and also Superintendent of Indian Affairs for the territory.[43]

Clark gave York his freedom and reportedly helped him to get started in a freight-hauling business with a wagon and a team of six horses. Shortly thereafter, in about 1820, York died in Tennessee apparently from cholera. Since he was about the same age as his master, he probably was about fifty years old.[44]

During the years that encompassed the lives of the members of the permanent party, birth and death rates were high, infant mortality rates were high, sanitation levels were low, diseases were rampant, and the level of health care and medical expertise was low, particularly when judged by modern standards. The new Republic was undergoing growing pains at every turn as it adjusted to the heady reality of the Louisiana Territory acquisition, which more than doubled the size of the United States. Most Americans were living lives of uncertainty, many as settlers, in unfamiliar, often dangerous conditions. Yet the members of the Lewis and Clark Expedition experienced conditions that were even more precarious and still lived considerably longer than the general populace of this era.

Low life expectancies, high death rates, high birth rates and high infant mortality rates had been the rule during Colonial times (and European health statistics were much worse).[45] In 1789, at the end of the Revolutionary War, life expectancy was 34.5 years for men and 36.5 for women, perhaps largely a reflection of high infant and child mortality rates. Sexagenarians in 1789 could look forward to 14.8 more years of life.[46] This fact illustrates the long-accepted actuarial principle that the longer one lives, the longer one can expect to live.

By comparing the foregoing data with that for the members of the expedition (average life span, 55-57 years; range, 32-99), it can be seen that their life spans far exceeded the life expectancies for people of their era. Except for John Shields and George Shannon, all of the members of the corps (for whom data are available) had been born in the 1770s. One reason for their longevity is that these men were not representative of the average young men of this period. They had been carefully selected by the captains for their hardiness, their shooting and hunting skills, their physical strength, and perceived ability to withstand a long journey in the wilderness. Also, by the time of their induction, as young adults, they had already survived the precarious stages of infancy and early childhood when mortality rates had been very high.

Participation in the expedition probably did not lower the life spans of the men. Encompassing twenty-eight months, the trip represented a relatively brief portion of their total life span. However, had it lasted much longer, and had the conditions continued, the men soon would have become unable to continue with the expedition because of health problems. Their chronic dietary lacks and strenuous exertions already were taking their toll. And the exorbitantly high protein intake associated with their high meat consumption soon would have resulted in serious dysfunctions of the gastrointestinal organs, liver, and kidneys. Beginning in late summer 1805, the decreasing health and hardiness of the men became increasingly evident.

Followers of the Lewis and Clark Expedition frequently express wonder that the men who had been so ailing during the winter at Fort Clatsop should revive so suddenly, appearing to be well and ready to depart up the Columbia on March 23, 1806, bound for home. In fact, not all of the members of the corps were completely well on the day of departure. William Bratton, for example, still had a severe back condition, dating back to the previous summer. He still was suffering from it in April, some weeks later, going overland from the Dalles to the open prairie. So he was allowed to ride on one of the party's ten horses. Very likely the prospect of going home gave many of the men a so-called "adrenaline rush." And, with the end of the expedition now clearly in sight, each of them probably summoned his last ounce of energy to make it happen. Almost any dreaded experience can be tolerated if one believes that it will not last long. As they wended their way homeward, other things, too, were working in their favor. At last, they now were out in the fresh air, no longer living under crowded conditions of Fort Clatsop. And now that it was spring the sun was shining, with its bactericidal effect and its ability to convert the ergosterol and 7-dehydrocholesterol in their diets to vitamin D. One of the key reasons for the success of the expedition may have been the fact that, most of the time, the party was on the move.

The men were incredibly lucky at various critical junctures during the trip, when the expedition easily could have failed had things happened a bit differently. Somehow, the party always managed to obtain food before its scarcity had a chance to inflict irreversible damage. Despite being caught in storms on the water, snow storms while going over the Bitterroots, and slipping while trying to go up steep mountain sides, suffering dislocated shoulders and other injuries, they managed to come out of these experiences alive, quickly regaining their ability to function. Probably all of them were leaner at the end of the journey than at the beginning, in May of 1804. Their ability to find their way through unfamiliar territory was uncanny. Finally, it is miraculous that the captains, by treating the afflicted men with their limited medical supplies, were able to heal them sufficiently to become participating crew members again.

From the moment they began to plan for the expedition, the captains had been aware that the corps would have to eat primarily off the land. They realized that every day would involve the search for food. Indeed, this quest continued throughout the trip. Getting enough food has always been man's top priority, followed by the need to obtain enough of the right kinds of food to supply the body with sufficient amounts of specific nutrients.

At the time of their recruitment in late 1803, because of the careful selectivity employed by Lewis and Clark, the men were healthier and in better condition than most Americans during the early years of the new Republic. Moreover, during their stay at Camp Dubois the winter before departure, the men had access to sufficient food, both from hunting and from nearby army commissaries. However, like most Americans of this era, their diets had certain faults. Fat, salt, and sugar consumption tended to be high. In addition, their intakes of riboflavin, vitamin C, vitamin E, folic acid, calcium, and fiber probably were low. And because of the iodine-poor soils of their native habitats their iodine consumption was inadequate. Adults during this era drank essentially no milk. Moreover, since the journals make virtually no mention of milk consumption by the men while at Camp Dubois, calcium consumption must have been low. They had been eating plenty of protein and carbohydrates but had been lacking in fresh fruits and vegetables and eggs. Thus, they probably were deficient in folic acid, riboflavin, and vitamins C and E.

Once the men embarked on the expedition proper, their diets changed, depending on the foods available within each ecosystem they encountered. At times, their overriding nutritional problem was lack of food *per se* (e.g., going over the Bitterroots.) Most of the dietary deficiencies which they had upon embarking on the expedition tended to remain, and often became exacerbated. One tangible improvement in their diet was that the men's sugar consumption went down. They had departed Wood River with just 112 pounds of sugar (Table 5.1), which appears to have constituted the total amount used by the party throughout the trip. Their copious consumption of meat during the summer of 1805 was clearly unhealthful.

Going up the Missouri toward Mandan country, the men suffered mainly from mild health complaints, such as sore eyes and constipation. Unfortunately, one man, Sergeant Charles Floyd, had died in August 1804 from a ruptured appendix and subsequent peritonitis.

The party left Mandan in April 1805 after a winter of moderate health problems (including some cases of venereal disease) and intermittent periods of feast and famine. As they resumed their voyage up the Missouri, the men appeared to do well for about two months. But by early June the rigors and stresses of the trip, plus their nutritional deficiencies, began to effect noticeable changes in their health. At the Marias River, Captain Lewis noted that the men had lost weight. In addition, many of the men were experiencing other health problems. Sacagawea became ill with a fever, probably due to pelvic inflammatory disease. By the time they reached Three Forks, the group was nearly immobilized by health problems, which included constipation, biliousness, tumors, boils, and injuries.

As the corps proceeded on toward the Pacific, its stresses continued, including intermittent periods of food scarcity, particularly while going over the Bitterroot Mountains. Once it became settled at Fort Clatsop, the party enjoyed a reasonably adequate food supply of deer, elk, fish, and wapato roots. Fortunately, the wapato roots agreed with the men much better than the camas roots that they had obtained from the Nez Perce in 1805. But their general ill health continued. This circumstance undoubtedly was a paramount factor in the captains' decision to depart for home somewhat sooner than originally planned, on March 23, 1806.

The road back was easier than the way out, mainly because the party now was revisiting familiar territory. And by crossing the Divide during the summer, the men avoided the problems of snow and cold weather encountered the previous winter of 1805.

Throughout the expedition, the party's consumption of riboflavin, vitamins C and E, folic acid, and calcium, plus fiber and water was generally lower than it had been prior to departure. These nutritional deficits were increased further by the various stresses which they encountered en route, since stress tends to increase the excretion of virtually all nutrients. An ongoing stress was the unpredictability of so many factors associated with the trip. For example, the men were under constant pressure to obtain food from the different environments through which they passed. In addition, there were the stresses of physical exertion, temperature extremes, stark danger, accidents, and physiological stresses (e.g., dehydration, undernutrition, and overnutrition). The net result of stress is that it increases the body's nutrient needs. Unfortunately, the members of the Lewis and Clark Expedition were experiencing high stresses at a time when their nutrient intakes were far from ideal. It is amazing that, despite their tribulations, the men retained much of their youthful resilience. However, considering their increasing health problems and decreasing ability to function, it is fortunate that the party departed for home on March 23, 1806, arriving safely at St. Louis on September 22, 1806.

Of the many factors which were responsible for the success of the expedition, the following would seem to be paramount: its excellent leadership; reasonably good medical care, resulting in only one death; the relative youth of the men; and the fairly short duration of the trip, which spanned twenty-eight months. Finally, throughout the expedition, the corps had enjoyed lots of luck.

Glossary

bark referring to Peruvian bark; cinchona, which contains quinine and quinidine

bee tree a tree which has attracted many bees, usually because it is nectar-bearing

biscuit a thin, flat, British cookie or cracker, with high keeping qualities due to its dryness and lack of shortening and leavening agents

biscuit-root *Peucedanum ambiguum*, also known as cows by the Spokane Indians; occurs principally in the Rocky Mountains west to the Pacific; noteworthy because of the edible tuberous roots of several species

bitterroot a plant, *Lewisia rediviva*, of western North America, having showy pink or white flowers and a starchy, edible root

blood pudding a black-colored sausage, usually made from hog's blood, bread crumbs, suet and oatmeal; also known as blood sausage

Blue Camas *Camassia quamash* (Pursh) Greene (also called *Camassia esculenta*), and *C. leichtlinii* (Baker) Wats; plants of the Liliaceae family; roots (bulbs) were a staple for the North American Indians, especially the Nez Perces and the Coast Salish of southern Vancouver Island

Boudin blanc French term for white pudding (sausage); a Cajun sausage

bread a food baked from a dough or batter made with flour or meal, water (or other liquid), and a leavening agent

bread of cows refers to a bread product made by the Indians from the biscuit-root by drying, then pulverizing the inside portion, mixing it with water and flattening it into cakes, which were dried in the sun or baked before eating; said to taste like stale biscuits

breadroot a plant, *Psoralea esculenta*, of the central North American plains, having an edible, starchy root; also called "prairie turnip," or "wild apple"

butter cracker a thin, crisp wafer or biscuit made of unleavened, unsweetened dough, containing butter as a shortening

camas see Blue Camas, White Camas

canning the act, process, or business of preserving foods in metal or glass containers, which are then subjected to high temperatures to destroy micro-organisms which cause spoilage; the sealed environment also eliminates oxidation and retards decomposition

cholera an acute bacterial enteric disease characterized in its severe form with sudden onset, profuse painless watery stools, occasional vomiting, and, in untreated cases, rapid dehydration, renal failure; if untreated, death frequently ensues

chronic disease a disease not transmissable, of a month's duration or longer

commissary a store where food and equipment are sold, as at a military post

common cold a viral infection of the respiratory tract, causing an acute inflammation of the nasal mucous membranes, marked by one or more of the following symptoms: discharge of mucus, sneezing, watering of the eyes, sore throat, and cough

contagious disease a disease transmissable by direct or indirect contact

contractor one who agrees to furnish materials or perform services at a specified price

crumpet a small, thin, round, yeast-leavened British batter bread baked on a griddle or stove top, similar to an English muffin

Death Camas see White Camas

decoctions extracts obtained by removing flavor or active principles by boiling plant products (leaves, fruit)

Delways referring to the Delaware Indians, a group of Algonquin-speaking North American tribes, formerly inhabiting the Delaware River Valley in the northeastern United States

diarrhea excessive evacuation of watery stools (feces)

dysentery an infection of the lower intestinal tract producing pain, fever, and severe diarrhea, often with blood and mucus

dyspepsia a catch-all term for stomach pains, upsets, and disorders of all kinds; indigestion

emetic 1. causing vomiting; 2. an agent or medicine which causes vomiting

empyem a pus in a body cavity, as in the pleural cacity, or gallbladder

endemic refers to the constant presence of a disease or infectious agent within a given geographic area or group of people

enema the injection of liquid into the rectum for cleansing, laxative, or other therapeutic purposes

engagé(és) French word, referring to the French/Indian boatmen who were hired for the Lewis and Clark Expedition

epidemic refers to a contagious disease that spreads rapidly, resulting in cases of an illness within a region with a frequency clearly in excess of normal expectancy

fennel 1. seeds have a weak, anise-like flavor and aroma and are used in baked goods, and savory dishes; 2. roots used by Lewis and Clark Expedition (Captain Clark's journal entry of May 16, 1806, noted that Sacagawea gathered a "quantity of fenel roots which we find very paliatiable and nurushing food."

fesic term used by Lewis and Clark for "physic," a lay term for laxative or cathartic

fish gigs 1. an arrangement of barbless hooks that is dragged through a school of fish to hook them in the bodies; 2. a pronged spear for fishing

floats floating objects which keep a seine from sinking

flint a very hard, fine-grained quartz that sparks when struck with steel, used for starting fires before matches were available

gangrene death and decay of tissue in a part of the body, usually a limb, due to failure of blood supply, injury, or disease

goiter a chronic noncancerous enlargement of the thyroid gland, visible as a swelling at the front of the neck, occurring without hyperthyroidism, and associated with iodine deficiency; endemic in regions where the soil is low in iodine, and sporadically elsewhere

gonorrhea an infectious disease of the genitourinary tract, rectum, and cervix, and characterized by acute purulent urethritis and painful or difficult urination; caused by a gonococcus, transmitted by sexual intercourse

griddle a flat pan or other flat metal surface used to fry foods; available with a long handle or two hand grips

grouse any of various plump birds of the family *Tetraonidae,* chiefly of the Northern hemisphere, having mottled brown or grayed plumage

hard tack hard, coarse unleavened bread traditionally used as army or navy rations because of its long shelf life; also known as sailor's biscuit or sea biscuit

hash a main dish of chopped meat, potatoes, and sometimes vegetables, usually browned and baked

heath hens a form of the prairie chicken *Tempanuchus cupido* that became extinct in eastern North America during the first part of the twentieth century

hulled grain grain from which the dry outer covering has been removed

immunity protection against infectious disease; being insusceptible to a disease

Indian meal ground meal made from corn; another word for cornmeal

Indian sweat a treatment used by the Choppunish Indians for paralyis and other maladies, which involved prolonged sweating within a special enclosed chamber

influenza an acute infectious viral disease characterized by inflammation of the respiratory tract, fever, muscular pain (myalgia), and irritation of the intestinal tract, general weakness and prostration; grippe

jerky thin strips of meat, usually best dried in the sun or oven; has a tough, chewy texture

Kickapoos members of a tribe of Algonquin-speaking Indians formerly of northern Illinois and southern Wisconsin

laxative a drug or medicine that stimulates evacuation of the bowels; a cathartic

leavening agent a substance used to produce or stimulate production of carbon dioxide in baked goods to impart a light texture

libation a beverage, usually alcoholic

lyed corn corn which has been treated with lye (sodium hydroxide) or the liquid obtained by leaching wood ashes, resulting in the removal of the hulls

malnutrition poor nutrition due to insufficient or poorly balanced diet, or because of defective digestion, absorption, or poor utilization of ingested foods

malaria a parasitic disease transmitted by the bites of an infective female Anolpheles mosquito; symptoms of the most serious malarial infection, falciparum malaria, may include fever, chills, sweats, cough, diarrhea, respiratory distress, and headache, progressing to more serious symptoms, and ending in death; fatalities of untreated cases exceed 10%

ophthalmia inflammation of the eye, especially the conjunctiva; conjunctivities marked by redness of the eyes and a slight exudate for a few days

parch to dry or roast corn, peas, or the like by exposing to heat

pelvic inflammatory disease (P.I.D.) infection of the fallopian tubes; a term sometimes wrongly used to include infections of the cervix, uterus, or the ovaries

pemmican a mixture of buffalo or venison, melted fat, berries and sometimes marrow, compressed into a small cake and dried

peritonitis inflammation of the peritoneum (the membrane lining the walls of the abdominal cavity, which covers most of the internal organs contained therein)

pleurisy inflammation of the pleura, the serous membrane sourrounding the lungs

pneumonia a disease marked by inflammation of the lungs which is usually caused by bactera (pneumococci) or by viruses

purgative a medicine used to evacuate the bowels; laxative or cathartic

purge to induce evacuation of the bowels in a patient

rabbit berry also known as bearberry; a trailing shrub, *Archtostaphylos uvaursi*, of northern regions, having small evergreen leaves, white or pink flowers, and red berries

rheumatism any of several pathological conditions of the muscles, tendons, bones, or nerves, characterized by discomfort and disability

Rush's pills a purgative consisting of calomel (mercurous chloride) and jalap, recommended by Dr. Benjamin Rush

sawyer one employed at sawing wood, as in a lumber camp or sawmill

scone a traditional Scottish quick bread originally made with oats and cooked on a griddle

scurvy a disease caused by a deficiency of vitamin C, characterized by spongy and bleeding gums, bleeding under the skin, extreme weakness, and slow wound healing

seine a large fishing net made to hang vertically in the water by weights at the lower edge and floats at the top

sepsis the presence of pathogenic (disease-producing) organisms, or their toxins, in the blood or tissues

shortening a fat such as butter, lard, or vegetable oil used to make baked goods light or flaky

simple a medicinal plant or the medicine obtained from it

skillet a frying pan; a round pan with a single long handle and low, sloping sides, used to pan-fry foods

smallpox also called variola; one of the most virulent infectious diseases which are transmitted man to man; one attack of smallpox protects against subsesequent attacks; main control is through vaccination; fatality can range between 1 and 30%

soup a liquid food prepared from meat, fish, or vegetable stock, sometimes combined with milk or a cream sauce, with various other ingredients added as pieces of solid food, and served either hot or cold

spider a cast-iron frying pan with a long handle and three legs that stands over a bed of coals in the hearth; a skillet with feet

splint to support or restrict, as with a sharp. slender piece of wood

staples certain foods which form the basis of a regional or national cuisine; the principal components of a diet

stew any food prepared by simmering or boiling slowly, usually containing meat and vegetables

syphilis a chronic infectious venereal disease caused by a spirochete, *Treponema pallidum*, transmitted by direct contact, usually by sexual intercourse

truss to secure poultry or other food with string, skewers, or pins so that it maintains its shape during cooking

typhoid fever a systemic bacterial disease characterized by insidious onset of sustained fever, severe headache, malaise, anorexia, a relative bradycardia, splenomegaly, rose spots on the trunk in 25% of white patients, nonproductive cough in the early stages of the illness, and constipation; more common than diarrhea (in adults); fatality rate of 10% can be reduced to <1% with prompt antibiotic therapy

typhus fever a louseborne rickettsial disease, marked by headache, chills, prostration, fever and general pains, followed by a spotty skin eruption; without specific therapy, fatality rate varies from 10 to 40%; last outbreak in United States occurred in 1921.

unleavened referring to a baked product to which a leavening agent has not been added

venereal disease a disease transmitted by sexual intercourse

yellow fever an acute infectious viral disease transmitted by mosquitos, of short duration and varying severity; produces jaundice, imparting a yellow appearance to the skin, and dark-colored vomit resulting from hemorrhages

voyager's grease a mixture of buffalo grease and tallow, commonly used in the making of pemmican

wapato an aquatic plant, known as the Arrowhead (*Sagittaria variabilis*, Eng.), so called from the shape of its leaves, found in wetlands throughout North America, valued universally by Indian tribes for its starchy, white tubers (bulbs)

White Camas also known as Death Camus (*Zigadenus venenosus*, Wats); of the Liliaceae family; its bulbs are poisonous, thus inedible; bulbs and leaves resemble those of Blue Camas, with which it frequently grows

wild apple see breadroot

NOTES

Introduction

[1] Stephen E. Ambrose, *Undaunted Courage* (New York: Simon & Schuster, Inc., 1996), pp. 74-75.

[2] Alexander Mackenzie, *The Journal of the Voyage to the Pacific*. Walter Sheppe, ed. (New York: Dover Publications, 1995), p. 305.

[3] United States Department of Agriculture, Human Nutrition Services. *Preparing foods and planning menus using the Dietary Guidelines*. (Washington: USGPO, 1989), 232-8: 11.

[4] United States Department of Agriculture, Human Nutrition Services. *The Food Pyramid*. Home and Garden Bulletin 252 (Washington: USGPO, 1992).

Chapter 1: Diet and Health in the Colonies and New Republic

[1] Elaine N. McIntosh, *American Food Habits in Historical Perspective* (Westport: Praeger, 1995), p. 72.

[2] James K. Martin, "Colonial Life in America" *World Book Encyclopedia*, 1989, 4: 796-97.

[3] Ibid., p. 797.

[4] C. Van Syckle, "Some pictures of food consumption in the United States: Part I, 1630-1860," *Journal of the American Dietetic Association* 19: 508 (1945).

[5] James K. Martin, pp. 797-98.

[6] Harvey A. Levenstein, *Revolution at the Table* (New York: Oxford University Press, 1988), p. 6.

[7] Sidney W. Mintz, "Pleasure, Profit, and Satiation." In Herman J. Viola and Caroline Margolis, *Seeds of Change* (Washington: Smithsonian Institution, 1991), p. 126.

[8] Sidney W. Mintz, *Sweetness and Power* (New York: Viking, 1985), p. 188.

[9] R.W. Fogel, S.L. Engerman, and J. Trussell, "Exploring the uses of data on height," *Social Sciences History* 7 (4): 415 (1982).

[10] Elaine N. McIntosh, p. 212.

[11] Waverly Root and Richard de Rochemont, *Eating in America* (Hopewell, NJ: Ecco Press, 1995), p. 356.

[12] John J. Hanlon and George E. Pickett, *Public Health* (St. Louis: Times Mirror/Mosby, 1984), p. 29.

[13] James K. Martin, p. 798.

[14] Eldon G. Chuinard, *Only One Man Died* (Glendale: Arthur Clark Co., 1979), p. 61.

[15] John W. Verano and Douglas H. Ubelaker, "Health and Disease in the Pre-Columbian World." In Herman J. Viola and Caroline Margolis, *Seeds of Change* (Washington: Smithsonian Institution, 1991), p. 223.

[16] Eldon G. Chuinard, p. 142.

[17] Ibid., p. 103.

[18] "Jefferson's instructions to Lewis, June 20, 1803." In Donald Jackson, ed., *Letters of the Lewis and Clark Expedition* (Urbana: University of Illinois Press, 1962), p.64.

[19] Lewis to Jefferson, October 3, 1803. Ibid., p. 130.

[20] Eldon G. Chuinard, p. 178.

[21] Norge W. Jerome, "The U.S. dietary pattern from an anthropological perspective," *Food Technology* 35 (2): 39-40, 1981.

[22] E.W. Martin, *The Standard of Living in 1860* (Chicago: University of Chicago Press, 1942), pp. 54-55; C. Volney, *View of the Climate and Soil of the United States of America* (London: J. Johnson, 1804), p. 323.

[23] Richard O. Cummings, *The American and His Food* (rev.). (New York, Arno Press, 1970), p. 15.

[24] H. Kephart, *Our Southern Highlanders* (New York: Macmillan, 1929), p. 16.

[25] Elaine N. McIntosh, p. 82.

[26] Ibid.

[27] H. Martineau, *Society in America*. II. (London, Saunders and Otley, 1837), pp. 44, 49.

[28] D.T. Lutes, *The Country Kitchen*, (Boston: Little, Brown, 1936), 211-12.

[29] Elaine N. McIntosh, p. 83.

[30] P. L. Ford, ed., *The Writings of Thomas Jefferson*. III. (New York: G.P. Putnam's Sons, 1894), p. 271.

[31] Elaine N. McIntosh, p. 85.

[32] T. De Voe, *The Market Assistant* (New York: Hurd and Houghton, 1867), pp. 104-5.

[33] A.W. Brayley, *Bakers and Baking Bread in Massachusetts* (Boston: Master Baker's Association of Massachusetts, 1909), pp. 122-4.

[34] Richard O. Cmmmings, pp. 27-29.

[35] Elaine N. McIntosh, p. 85.

[36] Richard O. Cummings, p. 34.

[37] Elaine N. McIntosh, pp. 86.

[38] Richard O. Cummings, 1970, Appendix C.

[39] R.W. Fogel, et al., pp. 415-16.

[40] Elaine N. McIntosh, pp. 213-14.

[41] C. Volney, *View of the Climate and Soil of the United States of America*. (London: J. Johnson, 1804), pp. 226-27; J.L. Mesick, *The English Traveler in America*. (New York: Columbia University Press, 1922), p. 90.

[42] C. Volney, p. 323.

[43] Elaine N. McIntosh, p. 214.

[44] Ibid.

[45] Richard O. Cummings, p. 17.

[46] Thomas Ashe, *Travels in America in 1806* (London: R. Phillips, 1808), p. 241.

[47] Waverly Root and Richard de Rochemont, p. 377.

[48] W.J. Rorabaugh, *The Alcoholic Republic* (New York: Oxford University Press, 1979), p. 125.

[49] Ibid.

[50] Eldon G. Chuinard, p. 135.

[51] John J. Hanlon and George E. Pickett, p. 30.

[52] Eldon G. Chuinard, p. 175; Edward F. Maguire, "Frequent Diseases and Intended Remedies on the Frontier (1780-1859)," Unpublished Master's Thesis, St. Louis University, 1953, p. 6.

Chapter 2: The Frontier Army Mess

[1] Barbara K. Luecke, *Feeding the Frontier Army* (Eagan, Minnesota: Grenadier Publications, 1994), p. 1.

[2] Dennis and Carol Farmer, *The King's Bread, 2nd Rising* (Youngstown, NY: Old Fort Niagara Association, Inc., 1989), pp. 14-15.

[3] Barbara K. Luecke, p. 3.

[4] Dennis and Carol Farmer, p. 74.

[5] Barbara K. Luecke, p. 1

[6] Lewis to Clark, June 19th, 1803. Donald Jackson, ed., *Letters of the Lewis and Clark Expedition with Related Documents* (Urbana: University of Illinois Press, 1962), p. 58.

[7] Elaine N. McIntosh, *American Food Habits in Historical Perspective* (Westport: Praeger, 1995), p. 89.

[8] Barbara K. Luecke, p. 10.

[9] Ibid., p. 12.

[10] Ibid., pp. 12; 14.

[11] Ibid., p. 16.

[12] Ibid, pp. 18; 20.

[13] Ibid., p. 20.

[14] Ibid., p. 25.

[15] Ibid., p. 30.

[16] Ibid., p. 126.

[17] Waverly Root and Richard de Rochemont, *Eating in America* (Hopewell, NJ: The Ecco Press, 1995), p. 225.

[18] William B. Skelton, *An American Profession of Arms: The Army Officer Corps, 1784-1861* (Lawrence: University Press of Kansas, 1992), p. 40.

[19] Gary E. Moulton, ed., *The Journals of the Lewis & Clark Expedition* (Lincoln: University of Nebraska Press, 1986,) vol. 2, p. 218. All further references to the expedition journals are from this edition.

[20] Alexander Mackenzie, *The Journal of the Voyage to the Pacific.* Walter Sheppe, ed. (New York: Dover Publications, 1995), pp. 17-18.

[21] Stephen E. Ambrose, *Undaunted Courage* (New York: Simon & Schuster, Inc., 1996), pp. 74-75.

[22] Gary E. Moulton, ed., p. 295, fn. 4; Grace Lee Nute, *The Voyageur* (1931; reprinted St. Paul: Minnesota Historical Society, 1955), p. 54.

Chapter 3: Medical Aspects of the Expedition

[1] Francis R. Packard, *History of Medicine in the United States* (New York: Paul B. Hoeber, Inc., 1931), p. 43.

[2] Eldon G. Chuinard, *Only One Man Died* (Glendale, Calif.: Arthur Clark Company, 1980), pp. 36-37.

[3] Ibid., p. 61

[4] Leon S. Bryan, Jr., "Blood-letting in American Medicine, 1803-1892." *Bulletin of the History of Medicine*, 38 (6): 516-29 (1964).

[5] Eldon G. Chuinard, p. 67.

[6] Jefferson to Benjamin Rush. In Donald Jackson, ed., *Letters of the Lewis and Clark Expedition, with Related Documents: 1783-1854* (Urbana: University of Illinois Press, 1962), p. 18.

[7] Eldon G. Chuinard, p. 122.

[8] David F. Hawke, *Benjamin Rush, Revolutionary Gadfly* (New York: Bobbs-Merrill Co., 1971), p. 326.

[9] Eldon G. Chuinard, pp. 140-41.

[10] Ibid., pp. 47-48; J.M. Toner, *The Medical Men of the Revolution* (Philadelpha: Collins Printer, 1876), p. 38.

[11] Eldon G. Chuinard, p. 159.

[12] Summary of Purchases: Donald Jackson, p. 97.

[13] Ibid., pp. 47; 88.

[14] Israel Wheelen's Bill for Portable Soup, May 30, 1803: Donald Jackson, p. 81.

[15] Edward Cutbush, *Observations on the Means of Preserving the Health of Soldiers* (Philadelphia: Fry and Kannerer,1808), pp. 314-15; Eldon G. Chuinard, p. 161.

[16] Eldon G. Chuinard, pp. 51-52; Eric Stone, *Medicine Among the American Indians* (New York: Cleo Medica; Paul B. Hoeber, Inc., 1932), p. 83.

[17] Eric Stone, Ibid.

[18] Eldon G. Chuinard, p. 52; Maurice B. Gordon, *Aesculapius Comes to the Colonies* (Ventor, NJ: Ventor Publishers, Inc., 1949).

[19] Bernard DeVoto, *The Journals of Lewis and Clark* (Boston: Houghton Mifflin, Co., 1953), p. 80.

[20] Albert F. Bennett, "Snake," *World Book Encyclopedia*, 1995, 17:527.

[21] Eldon G. Chuinard, pp. 52-53.

[22] Ibid., p. 56.

[23] Ibid., p. 49.

Chapter 4: Preparing for the Expedition

[1] James K. Hosmer, *History of the Expedition of Captains Lewis and Clark* (Chicago: A.C. McClurg & Co., 1917), p. xlvi.

[2] Gary E. Moulton, ed., *The Journals of the Lewis & Clark Expedition* (Lincoln: University of Nebraska Press, 1986), vol. 2, p. 65.

[3] James Villas, *My Mother's Southern Kitchen* (New York: Macmillan, 1994), pp. xi-xii.

[4] Gary E. Moulton, 1986 (2), p. 85.

[5] Ibid., p. 90, fn. 5.

[6] Ibid., p. 132, fn. 4. Apparently named Rivière à Dubois after a long-forgotten Frenchman.

[7] Ibid., p. 133, fn. 1. Most of the information regarding the party's stay at Camp Dubois has been obtained from the Field Notes of Captain Clark, in Moulton, 1986 (2).

[8] Gary E. Moulton, 1986(2), pp. 228-29, fn. 3.

[9] Paul S. Martin and Christine R. Szuter, "War Zones and Game Sinks in Lewis and Clark's West," *Conservation Biology* 13 (1): 36-45 (1999).

[10] Gary E. Moulton, 1986 (2), p. 215. Clark's journal entry, May 14, 1804.

[11] Clark's Field Notes, December 13, 1803-May 14, 1804, Moulton 1986 (2). All further references to the journals are from this edition.

[12] Gary E. Moulton, 1986 (2), p. 173. This is a rare instance of the party's having access to milk. In such a small amount, it must have been used only in coffee or tea. The only other mention of the party's obtaining milk occurred May 18, 1804, in the St. Charles area, ibid., p. 237.

[13] Ibid., p. 181.

[14] Ibid., pp. 181-82.

[15] Ibid., pp. 174-75.

[16] Elaine N. McIntosh, *American Food Habits in Historical Perspective* (Westport: Praeger, 1995), pp. 75, 83, 212, 215-16; Waverly Root and Richard de Rochemont, *Eating in America* (Hopewell, NJ: The Ecco Press, 1995), pp. 356-372.

[17] Gary E. Moulton, 1986 (2), pp. 178-179.

[18] Ibid., p. 203

[19] C. Anne Wilson, *Food and Drink in Britain* (Chicago: Academy Chicago Publishers, 1991), p. 232.

[20] James K. Martin, "Colonial Life in America," *World Book Encyclopedia*, 1995, 4: 807.

[21] Gary E. Moulton, 1986 (2), p. 234, fn. 4.

[22] Clark's behavior may appear to be compulsive here. But, considering his restricted amount of space, items had to be loaded thoughtfully for maximum convenience and efficiency en route, as well as for balance.

[23] Gary E. Moulton, 1986 (2), p. 215, fn. 2.

Chapter 5: From St. Louis to the Pacific and Back

[1] The captains committed a diplomatic *faux pas* in presenting these paltry gifts in return for the Indians' generous gifts of food.

[2] Again, perhaps too small a gift was given, considering the generosity of the Indians.

[3] Paul S. Martin and Christine R. Szuter, "War Zones and Game Sinks in Lewis and Clark's West," *Conservation Biology* 13 (1): 38 (1999).

[4] Bernard DeVoto, *The Journals of Lewis and Clark* (New York: Houghton Mifflin Company, 1953), pp. 107-08.

[5] Paul S. Martin and Christine R. Szuter, p. 39.

[6] In practice, the men must not have received one gill of liquor every day. Had the entire party of thirty-one men received that amount daily, it would have run out of liquor after 103 days, or about 3½ months en route (late August 1804.). In fact, they exhausted their liquor supply on July 4, 1805, at the mouth of the Yellowstone River.

[7] Gary E. Moulton, 1988 (5), p. 3.

[8] Bernard DeVoto, p. 249.

[9] James P. Ronda, *Lewis and Clark Among the Indians* (Lincoln: University of Nebraska Press, 1984), p. 178.

Chapter 6: Dietary and Health Assessment

[1] Lewis to Clark, August 3, 1803, pp. 115-17; Clark to Lewis, August 21, 1803, pp. 117-18: Donald Jackson, *Letters of the Lewis and Clark Expedition* (Urbana: University of Illinois Press, 1962), pp. 117-18.

[2] Lewis to Clark, June 19, 1803: Jackson, p. 58.

[3] R.W. Fogel, S.L. Engerman, and J. Trussell, "Exploring the uses of data on height." *Social Science History* 6 (4): 415 (1982).

[4] Captain Lewis was quartered in St. Louis during this time.

[5] Eldon G. Chuinard, *Only One Man Died* (Glendale: Arthur Clark Co., 1979), p. 238. The first appendectomy was performed in 1884 by Rudolf Kronlein (1847-1910).

[6] Gary E. Moulton, ed., *The Journals of the Lewis & Clark Expedition* (Lincoln: University of Nebraska Press, 1986), vol. 2, p. 173, fn. 2.

[7] Lewis to Jefferson, April 7, 1805: Jackson, pp. 231-34.

[8] Paul S. Martin and Christine R. Szuter, "War Zones and Game Sinks in Lewis and Clark's West," *Conservation Biology*, 13 (1): 38 (1999).

[9] Ronald V. Loge, "'Two dozes of barks and opium': Lewis and Clark as physicians," *The Pharos of Alpha Omega Alpha.* 59 (3): 26-31 (1996).

[10] Drake W. Will, "The Medical and Surgical Practice of the Lewis and Clark Expedition." *The Journal of the History of Medicine and Allied Sciences*, 14 (3): 290 (1959).

[11] Eldon G. Chuinard, p. 289.

[12] Bruce C. Paton, *Lewis and Clark: Doctors in the Wilderness* (Golden, Colorado: Fulcrum Publishing, 2001), p. 132.

[13] Howard J. Beard, "The Medical Observations and Practice of Lewis and Clark." *Scientific Monthly*, 20 (5): 506-26 (1925).

[14] D.R. Yesner, "Life in the 'Garden of Eden': causes and consequences of the adopting of marine diets by human societies." In M. Harris and E.B. Ross, eds., *Food and Evolution*. (Philadelphia: Temple University Press, 1987). pp. 285-310.

[15] Elaine N. McIntosh, *American Food Habits in Historical Perspective* (Westport: Praeger, 1995), p. 25.

[16] Bernard DeVoto, *The Journals of Lewis and Clark* (Boston: Houghton Mifflin Company, 1953), p. 241.

[17] Eldon G. Chuinard, p. 321

[18] Nancy J. Turner, *Food Plants of Coastal First Peoples* (Vancouver: University of British Columbia Press, 1995), pp. 139-40.

[9] Ibid., p. 140.

[20] Ibid., pp. 139-40.

[21] Ibid., p. 44.

[22] Ibid., p. 42.

[23] Eldon G. Chuinard, pp. 392-94.

Chapter 7: Food, Nutrition, and Health Aspects of the Expedition

[1] Paul S. Martin and Christine R. Szuter. "War Zones and Game Sinks in Lewis and Clark's West." *Conservation Biology*, 13 (1): 38 (1999).

[2] Ibid., pp. 38-39.

[3] Ibid., p. 40.

[4] Stephen E. Ambrose, *Undaunted Courage* (New York: Simon and Schuster, 1996), p. 294.

[5] Under Spanish rule, these Indians were forbidden to have guns.

[6] Elaine N. McIntosh, *American Food Habits in Historical Perspective* (Westport: Praeger, 1995), p. 25; D.R. Yesner, "Life in the 'Garden of Eden': causes and consequences of the adopting of marine diets by human societies." In M. Harris and E.B. Ross, eds., *Food and Evolution* (Philadelphia: Temple University Press, 1987), pp. 286-91.

[7] Frances Dahlberg, ed., *Woman the Gatherer* (New Haven: Yale University Press, 1981).

[8] Gary E. Moulton, *The Journals of the Lewis & Clark Expedition* (Lincoln: University of Nebraska Press, 1986), vol. 2, p. 509.

[9] Now known as the Lewis and Clark River.

[10] Gary E. Moulton, *The Journals of the Lewis & Clark Expedition* (Lincoln: University of Nebraska Press, 1990), vol. 6, p. 333. The salt processors were Joseph Fields, William Bratton, and George Gibson, assisted by other members of the corps, p. 140.

[11] Charles Francis Saunders, *Edible and Useful Wild Plants* (New York: Dover Publications Inc., 1948), p. 245.

[12] Harry F. Thompson, "Meriwether Lewis and His Son: The Claim of Joseph De Somet Lewis and the Problem of History," *North Dakota History* 67 (3): 24-37 (2000).

[13] Root vegetables also include potatoes (both sweet and white), turnips, and rutabagas.

[14] Paul S. Martin and Christine R. Szuter, p. 39.

[15] One ounce of medium-fat meat contains 75 kilocalories (i.e., energy), and 7 grams of protein. Thus, 4.5 pounds of meat would provide 5,400 kilocalories and 504 grams of protein. Nine pounds of meat would provide twice that—an incredible intake of 10,800 kilocalories and 1,008 grams of protein daily.

[16] Stephen E. Ambrose, p. 319.

[17] Fifer, Barbara and Vicky Sodereberg, *Along the Trail with Lewis and Clark*. (Great Falls, MT: Montana Magazine (printed by Advanced Litho Printing, 1998), p. 158. A reconstruction of the fort can be seen today at the Fort Clatsop National Memorial, near Astoria, Oregon.

[18] Gary E. Moulton, 1990 (6), p. 242. Moulton notes that because prolonged use of mercurous chloride, itself, can be poisonous, it could have been a factor in their early mortality.

[19] Only three of the men were formally cited in the journals as having venereal disease: George Gibson, Silas Goodrich, and Hugh McNeal. However, from general comments made in the journals, many more had also became infected.

[20] Gerald S. Snyder, *In the Footsteps of Lewis and Clark* (Washington, D.C.: National Geographic Society, 1970), p. 200.

[21] Eldon G. Chuinard, *Only One Man Died* (Glendale, Calif.: Arthur Clark Company, 1980), p. 181.

[22] Stephen E. Ambrose, pp. 109-10; 196.

[23] Ibid., p. 312; Gerald S. Snyder, p. 198.

[24] Jefferson to Paul Allen, August 18, 1813: Donald Jackson, pp. 591-92.

[25] Bernard DeVoto, *The Journals of Lewis and Clark* (New York: Houghton Mifflin Company, 1953), p. 92.

[26] Ibid., p. 90.

[27] Reuben Gold Thwaites, *Original Journals of the Lewis and Clark Expedition* (New York: Antiquarian Press Ltd., 1904-05, reprinted 1959), vol. 5, pp. 124-27.

[28] Gerald S. Snyder, p. 198.

[29] Ibid., p. 200; Stephen E. Ambrose, p. 399.

[30] National Archives, series M19, reel 189:150, from Carol L. MacGregor, *The Journals of Patrick Gass* (Missoula, MT: Mountain Press Publishing Company, 1997), p. 224, fn. 26; p. 424.

[31] Carol L. MacGregor, pp. 303-04; 424.

[32] Ibid., pp. 303-04, 440.

[33] Ibid., p. 304, paragraph 1; John G. Jacob, *The Life and Times of Patrick Gass* (Wellsburg, Va.: Jacob & Smith, 1859), pp. 176-77.

[34] Gary E. Moulton, 1986 (2), p. 524.

[35] Ibid., 1997 (11), p. xvi.

[36] Davis Thomas and Karin Ronnefeldt, eds., *People of the First Man* (New York: Promontory Press, 1982), p. 8; Gary E. Moulton, 1987 (3), p. 229.

[37] Gerald S. Snyder, p. 199

[38] Ibid., p. 200

[39] Reuben Gold Thwaites, vol. 1, xl.

[40] Dayton Duncan and Ken Burns, *Lewis and Clark* (New York: Alfred A. Knopf, 1997), p. 214.

[41] Ibid., p. 215.

[42] Ibid.

[43] Gerald S. Snyder, p. 198.

[44] Ibid., p. 199.

[45] Elaine N. McIntosh, p. 212; J.W. Verano and D.H. Ubelaker. "Health and Disease in the Pre-Columbian World." In Herman J. Viola and Caroline Margolis, *Seeds of Change* (Washington: Smithsonian Institution, 1991), p. 223.

[46] Richard O. Cummings, *The American and His Food,* rev. (New York: Arno Press, 1970), Appendix C.

Bibliography

Ambrose, Stephen E. *Undaunted Courage: Meriwether Lewis, Thomas Jefferson, and the Opening of the American West*. New York: Simon & Schuster, Inc., 1996.

Ashe, Thomas. *Travels in America in 1806*. London: R. Phillips, 1808.

Beard, Howard J., M.D. "The Medical Observations and Practice of Lewis and Clark." *Scientific Monthly*, 20 (5): 506-26 (1925).

Bennett, Albert. "Snake." *World Book Encyclopedia*, 17: 527 (1995).

Brayley, A.W. *Bakers and Baking Bread in Massachusetts*. Boston: Master Bakers's Association of Massachusetts, 1909.

Bryan, Leon S., Jr. "Blood-letting in American Medicine, 1803-1892." *Bulletin of the History of Medicine*, 38 (6): 516-29 (1964).

Chuinard, Eldon G. *Only One Man Died: The Medical Aspects of the Lewis and Clark Expedition*. Glendale: Arthur Clark Company, 1979.

Cummings, Richard O. *The American and His Food* (rev.). New York: Arno Press, 1970.

Cutbush, Edward. *Observations on the Means of Preserving the Health of Soldiers and Sailors*. Philadelphia: Fry and Kannerer, 1808.

Dahlberg, Frances, ed. *Woman the Gatherer*. New Haven: Yale University Press, 1981.

DeVoe, T. *The Market Assistant*. New York: Hurd and Houghton, 1867.

DeVoto, Bernard. *The Journals of Lewis and Clark*. Boston: Houghton Mifflin Company, 1953.

Duncan, Dayton and Ken Burns. *Lewis and Clark*. New York: Alfred A. Knopf, 1997.

Farmer, Dennis and Carol. *The King's Bread, 2nd Rising*. Youngstown, NY: Old Fort Niagara Association, Inc., 1989.

Fifer, Barbara and Vicky Soderberg. "Along the Trail with Lewis and Clark." Great Falls, MT: *Montana Magazine* (printed by Advanced Litho Printing, 1998).

Fogel, R.W., S.L. Engerman, and J. Trussell. "Exploring the uses of data on height." *Social Sciences History* 6 (4): 401-21 (1982).

Ford, P.L., ed. *The Writings of Thomas Jefferson, III*. New York: G.P. Putnam's Sons, 1894.

Gordon, Maurice B. *Aesculapius Comes to the Colonies*. Ventor, N.J.: Ventor Publishers, Inc., 1949.

Hanlon, John J. and George E. Pickett. *Public Health*. St. Louis: Times Mirror/Mosby, 1984.

Hawke, David F. *Benjamin Rush, Revolutionary Gadfly*. New York: Bobbs-Merrill Co., 1971.

Holland, Leandra. "Preserving Food on the Lewis and Clark Expedition." *We Proceeded On*, 27 (3): 6-11 (2001).

Hosmer, James K. *History of the Expedition of Captains Lewis and Clark*. Paul Allen, ed. Chicago: A.C. McClurg & Co., 1917.

Jackson, Donald, ed. *Letters of the Lewis and Clark Expedition, with Related Documents: 1783-1854*. Urbana: University of Illinois Press, 1962.

Jacob, John G. *The Life and Times of Patrick Gass, Now Sole Survivor of the Overland Expedition to the Pacific, under Lewis and Clark, in 1804-5-6*. Wellsburg, Va.: Jacob & Smith, 1859.

Jerome, Norge W. "The U.S. dietary pattern from an anthropological perspective." *Food Technology*, 35 (2): 39-40 (1981).

Kephart, H. *Our Southern Highlanders*. New York: Macmillan, 1929.

Levenstein, Harvey A. *Revolution at the Table*. New York: Oxford University Press, 1988.

Loge, Ronald V. "'Two dozes of barks and opium': Lewis and Clark as physicians." *The Pharos of Alpha Omega Alpha*, 59 (3): 26-31 (1996).

Luecke, Barbara K. *Feeding the Frontier Army*. Eagan, Minnesota: Grenadier Publications, 1994.

Lutes, D.T. *The Country Kitchen*. Boston: Little, Brown, 1936.

MacGregor, Carol L. *The Journals of Patrick Gass*. Missoula, MT: Mountain Press Publishing Company, 1997.

Mackenzie, Alexander. *Journal of the Voyage to the Pacific*. Walter Sheppe, ed. New York: Dover Publications, 1995.

Maguire, Edward F. "Frequent Diseases and Intended Remedies on the Frontier (1780-1850)." Unpublished Master's Thesis, St. Louis University, 1953.

Martin, E.W. *The Standard of Living in 1860*. Chicago: University of Chicago Press, 1942.

Martin, James K. "Colonial Life in America." *World Book Encyclopedia*, 4:796-807 (1989).

Martin, Paul S., and Christine R. Szuter. "War Zones and Game Sinks in Lewis and Clark's West," *Conservation Biology,* 13 (1): 36-45 (1999).

McIntosh, Elaine N. *American Food Habits in Historical Perspective.* Westport: Praeger, 1995.

Mesick, J.L. *The English Traveler in America, 1785-1835.* New York: Columbia University Press, 1922.

Mintz, Sidney W. *Sweetness and Power.* New York: Viking, 1985.

———. "Pleasure, Profit, and Satiation." In Herman J. Viola and Caroline Margolis, *Seeds of Change: A Quincentennial Commemoration.* Washington: Smithsonian Institution Press, 1991, pp. 112-29.

Moulton, Gary E. *The Journals of the Lewis & Clark Expedition.* Lincoln: University of Nebraska Press, Volumes 2-11, 1986-1997.

National Archives, series M19, reel 189:150. In Carol L. MacGregor, *The Journals of Patrick Gass.* Missoula, MT: Mountain Press Publishing Company, 1997, p. 224.

Nute, Grace Lee. *The Voyageur.* (1931). St. Paul: Minnesota Historical Society, 1955.

Packard, Francis R. *History of Medicine in the United States.* New York: Paul B. Hoeber, Inc., 1931.

Paton, Bruce C. *Lewis & Clark: Doctors in the Wilderness.* Golden, Colorado: Fulcrum Publishing, 2001.

Ronda, James P. *Lewis and Clark Among the Indians.* Lincoln: University of Nebraska Press, 1984.

Root, Waverly and Richard de Rochemont. *Eating in America.* Hopewell, NJ: Ecco Press, 1995.

Rorabaugh, W.J. *The Alcoholic Republic.* New York: Oxford University Press, 1979.

Saunders, Charles Francis. *Edible and Useful Wild Plants of the United States and Canada.* New York: Dover Publications, Inc., 1948.

Schaefer, J. *The Social History of American Agriculture.* New York: Macmillan, 1936.

Skelton, William B. *An American Profession of Arms: The Army Officer Corps, 1784-1861.* Lawrence: University Press of Kansas, 1992.

Smith, David T., and Donald S. Martin. *Zinsser's Textbook of Bacteriology.* New York: Appleton-Century Crofts, Inc., 1948.

Snyder, Gerald S. *In the Footsteps of Lewis and Clark.* Washington: National Geographic Society, 1970.

Stone, Eric. *Medicine Among the American Indians.* New York: Cleo Medica; Paul B. Hoeber, Inc., 1932.

Thomas, Davis and Karin Ronnefeldt, eds. *People of the First Man.* New York: Promontory Press, 1982.

Thompson, Harry F. "Meriwether Lewis and His Son: The Claim of Joseph De Somet Lewis and the Problem of History." *North Dakota History,* 67 (3): 24-37 (2000).

Thwaites, Reuben G. *Original Journals of the Lewis and Clark Expedition. 1904-1905.* Vols. 1-7. New York: Antiquarian Press Ltd., 1959.

Toner, J.M. *The Medical Men of the Revolution.* Philadelphia: Collins Printer, 1876.

Turner, Nancy J. *Food Plants of Coastal First Peoples.* Vancouver: University of British Columbia Press, 1995.

United States Department of Agriculture, Human Nutrition Services. *Preparing Foods and Planning Menus Using the Dietary Guidelines.* Home and Garden Bulletin 232-8: 11. Washington: USGPO, 1989.

———. *The Food Pyramid.* Home and Garden Bulletin 252. Washington: USGPO, 1992.

Van Syckle, C. "Some pictures of food consumption in the United States: part I, 1630-1860." *Journal of the American Dietetic Association,* 19: 508 (1945).

Verano, John W., and Douglas H. Ubelaker. "Health and Disease in the Pre-Columbian World." In Herman J. Viola and Caroline Margolis, *Seeds of Change: A Quincentennial Commemoration.* Washington: Smithsonian Institution, 1991, pp. 209-23.

Villas, James. *My Mother's Southern Kitchen.* New York: Macmillan, 1994.

Volney, C. *View of the Climate and Soil of the United States of America.* London: J. Johnson, 1804.

Will, Drake W. "The Medical and Surgical Practice of the Lewis and Clark Expedition." *The Journal of the History of Medicine and Allied Sciences,* 14 (3): 290 (1959).

Wilson, C. Anne. *Food and Drink in Britain.* Chicago: Academy Chicago Publishers, 1991.

Yesner, D.R. "Life in the 'Garden of Eden': Causes and Consequences of the adopting of marine diets by human societies." In M. Harris and E.B. Ross, eds. *Food and Evolution.* Philadelphia: Temple University Press, 1987, pp. 285-310.

Index

About the Author

Elaine Nelson McIntosh is a registered dietitian (R.D.) with a Ph.D. in biochemistry, bacteriology, and bacterial physiology from Iowa State University. She also holds an M.A. from the University of South Dakota and an A.B. from Augustana College. She was born in Webster, South Dakota.

She has held teaching and research appointments at Sioux Falls College, the University of South Dakota, University of Illinois, and University of Wisconsin at Green Bay. Her publications include books, book chapters, and numerous articles in professional journals. Her book *American Food Habits in Historical Perspective* was published by Praeger in 1995. She also serves as a reviewer for two professional journals.

Since 1996, McIntosh has presented a series of papers on the topic of this present study at the Dakota Conference on Northern Plains History, Literature, Art, and Archaeology, sponsored by the Center for Western Studies of Augustana College. In 2001, she received an award for having given one of the four best papers at the Dakota Conference from among seventy presenters at the previous year's conference. In recognition of her career in nutrition education, McIntosh received the Augustana College Alumni Achievement Award in 2000.